LE

...f rms and...

Warwick Studies in Industrial Relations

The Docks after Devlin

Warwick Studies in Industrial Relations

General Editors: George Bain, Hugh Clegg,
Allan Flanders

Disputes Procedure in Action, R. Hyman
Race and Industrial Conflict, M. Rimmer
The Docks after Devlin, M. Mellish

The Docks after Devlin

A study of the effects of the recommendations of the
Devlin Committee on industrial relations
in the London docks

Michael Mellish

HEINEMANN EDUCATIONAL BOOKS
LONDON

Heinemann Educational Books Ltd

LONDON EDINBURGH MELBOURNE AUCKLAND TORONTO
HONG KONG SINGAPORE KUALA LUMPUR
IBADAN NAIROBI JOHANNESBURG
NEW DELHI

ISBN 0 435 85605 7

First published 1972

Published by
Heinemann Educational Books Ltd
48 Charles Street, London W1X 8AH

Printed in Great Britain by
Willmer Brothers Limited, Birkenhead

Editors' Foreword

Warwick University's first undergraduates were admitted in 1965. The teaching of industrial relations began a year later, and in 1967 a one-year graduate course leading to an M.A. in Industrial Relations was introduced. At about the same time a grant from the Clarkson Trustees allowed a beginning to be made on a research project concerned with several aspects of industrial relations in selected Coventry plants.

In 1970 the Social Science Research Council established three Research Units, one of them being the Industrial Relations Research Unit at Warwick. The Unit took over the Coventry project and developed others, including studies of union growth, union organization, occupational labour markets, coloured immigrants in industry, ideologies of 'fairness' in industrial relations and the effects of the Industrial Relations Act.

This monograph series is intended to form the main vehicle for the publication of the results of the Unit's projects, of the research carried out by staff teaching industrial relations in the University, and, where it merits publication, of the work of graduate students. Some of these results will, of course, be published as articles, and some in the end may constitute full-scale volumes. But the monograph is the most apt form for much of our work. Industrial relations research is concerned with assembling and analyzing evidence much of which cannot be succinctly summarized in tables and graphs, so that an adequate presentation of findings can easily take too much space for an article.

On the other hand, even with a major project which will in the end lead to one or more books, there is often an advantage in publishing interim results as monographs. This is particularly true where the project deals, as do several of the industrial relations studies at Warwick, with problems of current interest for which employers, trade unionists and governments are anxiously seeking solutions.

Mr Mellish's study reports the findings of a project of this kind. The docks, and above all the London docks, have been a trouble-spot in British industrial relations for nearly a century. The Devlin Committee were only the last of a series of bodies entrusted with finding a solution to the labour problems of the docks, although their recommendations were more far-reaching than those of most of their predecessors. These recommendations were generally in line with current ideas on the prevailing shortcomings of British industrial relations and their remedies, as exemplified, for instance, in the Donovan Report. Consequently the application of the Devlin proposals in the London docks involved testing ideas of reform which are thought to be relevant to many other industries besides the docks; and Mr Mellish's study should be of interest to everyone concerned with the reform of industrial relations whether as practitioners or students.

GEORGE BAIN
HUGH CLEGG
ALLAN FLANDERS

Contents

List of Tables

List of Graphs

List of Abbreviations

DE   Department of Employment
EDJIC   Enclosed Docks Joint Industrial Council
EDMC   Enclosed Docks Modernization Committee
LDLB   London Dock Labour Board
LOTEA   London Ocean Trades Employers' Association
NASDU   National Amalgamated Stevedores and
                Dockworkers Union
NDLB   National Dock Labour Board
OTGJC   Ocean Trade Group Joint Committee
PLA   Port of London Authority
PLAGJC   Port of London Authority, Group Joint
                Committee
TGWU (T & G)   Transport and General Workers Union

I

Introduction

The Devlin Committee[1] found industrial relations in the docks wanting. The central defect, they said, was the casual nature of employment. This bred casual management and reciprocal casual attitudes on the part of labour. It also caused insecurity in working conditions and this insecurity, according to the Committee, lay behind the high strike rate of the docks and their restrictive labour practices. These were taken to be the two prime indices of poor labour relations. The Committee also found that industrial relations in the docks were complicated by inter-union conflict and poor internal communication between the officers of the major dock union and its members. As a result its recommendations were aimed at changing the attitudes of management and labour, and at reforming union organization.

This is a study of the effects which the recommendations of the Devlin Committee had in London where they have been implemented in two stages. Phase 1 brought decasualization, the assigning of all docks workers to individual employers on a permanent basis. Phase 2 brought a review of port payment systems and the introduction of shiftwork.

Management
The Devlin Committee gave several examples of casual management and these may be broadly categorized, in

[1] *Final Report of the Devlin Committee on the Port Transport Industry*, 1965 HMSO, Cmnd. 2734.

London at least, into three types of managerial deficiency.
Firstly, employers showed an irresponsible attitude to labour
in hiring and dismissing men on a casual basis. Casual
labour, in one form or other, has been universal in the
docks. Because they were faced with a fluctuating demand,
employers followed a policy of taking on labour when it
was needed and laying it off when it was no longer required.
The Devlin Committee said this situation was wrong in
itself and also brought unpalatable results for the industry
by encouraging a parallel lack of responsibility among men
towards their employers. They thus recommended the
decasualization of dock work which meant that dockers
should be permanently employed by individual employers.
Phase 1 was designed to achieve this, but, until Phase 2,
the temporary transfer of employees was allowed, so that
in the meantime permanent employment was more permanent at some firms than others.

Secondly, in London at least, the employers limited
normal managerial responsibilities still further by operating
payment systems which placed the onus on workers to
maintain the pace of work and decide the best methods.
These piecework systems also minimized the wages that the
employers had to pay when work was temporarily unavail-
able. It was thus a natural corollary to the casual system
of hiring. Decasualization did not of itself alter the system
of payment, and traditional piecework systems were worked
during Phase 1; but the high cost of these incentive payment systems for a permanent labour force was an incentive to change. Decasualization also highlighted the way
these payment systems had stimulated daily negotiations
and led to a high incidence of strikes. The Devlin Committee
were aware of the deficiencies of payment systems in the
docks and recommended a review of the wage structure
and methods of pay in the industry. The move away from
piecework in Phase 2 of Devlin in London placed new
responsibilities on employers to supply dockers with a steady
flow of work and to organize its execution. Whatever the
state of work at their firms, a high basic wage had to be

paid to workers which gave no encouragement to work at any particular pace. Employers differed in their ability to meet these new responsibilities for organizing and supervising work.

Thirdly, as well as employing casually and operating payment systems which limited their own supervisory responsibilities, employers traditionally acquiesced in a wide range of practices which they considered restrictive to production. Whatever the historical origin of such practices and whatever the dockers' reasons for following them, this acquiescence further limited managements' day-to-day responsibility to decide the optimum number of men required to work a particular job and to choose the men who should make up the number. Thus when these practices were bought out by the Phase 2 settlement in London, employers were faced with further new responsibilities and once more it will be seen that not all employers were equipped or able to undertake them.

Much of this study is therefore devoted to examining and comparing the success of firms in decasualizing their methods of management.

Labour

The study is also concerned with changes in the attitudes and behaviour of dock workers. The casual attitudes and behaviour of dockers were ascribed by the Devlin Committee to the insecurity of casual employment. They recognized that there were two elements to this insecurity. Firstly, there was the uncertainty of getting a daily job at all. V. H. Jensen has said, 'it is well known that the method of hiring dock labour in Great Britain had left all the hardships from the fluctuating demand to be borne wholly by the casual men.'[1] A second source of insecurity was the dockers' fluctuating and uncertain earnings. This was due in part to underemployment, but it was also the product of the payment systems. This study shows that decasualiza-

[1] V. H. Jensen, *Hiring of Dock Workers*. (Cambridge, Mass: Harvard University Press, 1964), p. 122.

tion itself did not bring security in daily or weekly earnings in London. Despite permanent employment, wages fluctuated under Phase 1 as before because piecework systems continued as before. Meanwhile the closure of three sectors of the enclosed docks and several large wharfingers[1] brought a new element of insecurity to dock work. However, Phase 2 replaced piecework with a high basic wage and so removed the insecurity of fluctuating earnings.

Insecurity had built up two conflicting pressures among dock workers. Firstly, there was pressure to share work equally among all dockers. The evil of underemployment was traditionally compounded by the employers' favouritism towards some dockers (the 'blue-eyed boys' of the Devlin Report) at the expense of others. Dockers thus felt the need to present a common and solid front in the face of the fluctuating demand for their services and preferential treatment by employers. This led them, among other things, to maintain levels of manning and rules on the distribution of jobs aimed at spreading work and sharing it out fairly.

Somewhat paradoxically, fairness also demanded differential treatment for those workers whom the dockers recognized as having different skills or supplying different levels of effort. Under the casual system the industry did not have a wage structure which recognized differences in skill and effort, and decasualization itself did not change this. London dockers received a wage structure only with the Phase 2 agreement, and even this did not meet all their demands for fair differentials.

The insecurity of the casual system also encouraged dockers to exploit to the full the earning capacity of jobs when they had them, and piecework provided the opportunity. This opportunity declined when piecework was abolished in Phase 2. Hence another primary aim of this study is to discover the effect the two stages of decasualization on the attitudes and behaviour of dockers.

[1] See Appendix I.

Unions

The Devlin Committee found that industrial relations in the docks were complicated by inter-union conflict and poor communication between the major trade union and its members. The recommendations included a settlement between the unions on their respective spheres of influence, and a proposal that the major union should re-establish its power and authority by persuading its members that it had a sound policy and the means to carry it out. In the short term, a great campaign to improve its communications was thought necessary. In the longer term, the establishment of a shop steward system was seen as a necessary accompaniment to permanent employment, and as a means to improve union communications. Thus the third main objective of the study is to discuss the extent of union co-operation with the Devlin recommendations and the effect of decasualization upon the unions.

The Study

To find out the effect of the Devlin Committee's recommendations, the experiences of three firms in one sector of the London docks were compared. This was done in two periods, the summer of 1969 and the winter and spring of 1970–71. The findings apply only up to April 1971.

The study was limited to three firms in one sector, the Millwall and India sector, so as to allow shop floor industrial relations in the docks to be examined in some depth, with the Devlin recommendations as a focus. In each firm all senior managers and shop stewards were interviewed, along with a proportion of junior managers varying from one-third to two-thirds, and some of the dockers. The author also sat in on some negotiations and disputes. Records of joint meetings in three firms were studied, along with the minutes of shop stewards' meetings and works committee meetings in the two firms where they were available. Wherever they existed, figures of earnings and productivity and records of disputes were collected. In addition, a number of people outside the three firms were interviewed,

including union officials, officers of the London Ocean
Trades Employers' Association (LOTEA) and members of
the Industrial Relations staff of the Port of London Authority (PLA).

The three firms were the Millwall and South West India
Departments of the PLA, a private firm which is a member
of the LOTEA (Firm A) and a second private firm which
negotiates its own agreements outside the LOTEA
(Firm B). Given the range in size and type of operation in
the London Docks, no three firms could be typical. These
three were chosen to give examples of several types of dock
work and managerial arrangements, including conventional and mechanized work; work on board ship, on the
quay and in sheds; and situations where the employer
controls the whole sequence of dock operations as well as
those where he controls only some of them.

With between thirty and forty per cent of the enclosed
docks labour force in its employment, the PLA is the largest
employer in the port. Its responsibility for dock work varies
from sector to sector. At Tilbury it manages the full range
of operations at container terminals. In the Royals it is
responsible for quay work on exports only, delivering export
cargoes from road and rail transport through the sheds
to the ship's side. At Millwall and India it is also responsible
for delivering imports from the ship's side back through the
sheds to road and rail, and in addition at India (but not at
Millwall) it handles the unloading of import cargoes from
ships. Thus the full range of PLA dock work is not covered
here, but the departments chosen for study have the most
varied work content of all the PLA departments.

At Tilbury the private stevedores can be responsible for
the full range of dock work. Elsewhere their responsibilities
complement those of the PLA. In the Royals they load and
unload ships and deliver import cargoes through the sheds
to road and rail. At Millwall they load and unload ships
but handle no quay work; and at India their responsibility
is only for the loading of the ship. Consequently Firm A
is not typical of London stevedores in general, but its

operations are representative of the type of work under-taken by stevedores in the Millwall and India sector.

The agreements on the implementation of the Devlin report were negotiated on the employers' side by the PLA and the LOTEA. They covered almost the whole of the enclosed docks, but not Firm B, which was selected because it is untypical. It is widely considered one of the most pro-gessive firms in London, not only because of its extensive use of mechanical handling but also for its labour policies. It offered permanent employment to its regular followers prior to decasualization; it abolished piecework three years before the rest of the Port of London; and in June 1969 it intro-duced shiftwork and abolished daily overtime over a year before Phase 2 accomplished these things for the rest of London. Not surprisingly it is seen as a pacesetter, particu-larly for the sector in which it is situated. Its experience can usefully be compared with that of firms covered by port-wide agreements implementing the Devlin Committee's recommendations. Moreover, it is a shipping company, not a contracting stevedore; and it is also a terminal operator which means it is responsible for all the work done on its leased premises—ship loading and discharge, shed and quay work, and lorry loading and discharge. This is in contrast to most of the rest of London where the PLA is responsible for quay work and private stevedores for shipwork. The firm's experiences as a terminal operator can be contrasted with the traditional organization of work.

The remaining chapters set out the findings of the study in detail. The first two sections deal with the effect of Phase 1 and Phase 2 agreements on the two firms which were covered by them. The third section compares their experience with that of the firm outside the agreements. The final section deals with union structure and organiza-tion.

2

Decasualization of Dock Work

The Devlin Committee ascribed the strike-proneness and time-wasting practices of the docks to the insecurity of the casual system of working and the mutual lack of responsibility of workers and employers bred by the system. They therefore recommended decasualization.

In September 1967 the National Dock Labour Board assigned men to employers as permanent employees. Employers for their part were assigned to the particular sectors in which they usually operated. This placed responsibility for the provision of work on the employers, but provision was made for employers to borrow and lend employees to allow for fluctuations in demand. A daily meeting took place at the local offices of the Dock Labour Board at which representatives of the area's employers gave each other an assessment of labour requirements for the following day. If there was either insufficient work or an excess of work then the employers could lend and borrow.

Overall, decasualization led to an increase in employment for dockers. For 1967 as a whole, the size of the live register (men normally available for employment) was 20,511, while average daily labour requirements for the year were 17,483. This gives an average daily unemployment figure of over 3,000. For 1968 the live register was 18,424 and labour requirements were 17,639, giving an average daily unemployment figure of less than 800. For 1969 the live register was 16,560 and labour requirements

15,424, the average daily unemployment figure was 1,136.[1]

As well as examining the overall employment picture, it is necessary to look at individual firms' records to see if decasualization meant the same thing for different workers in different firms. In fact, individual firms had very different records of daily employment during Phase 1. Two measures were used to estimate this. First, 'dead' days, i.e. days when employees were sent home without work; second, days on loan, when an employee was lent to another employer. Both measures together give an estimate of the time employees spent away from their firm. This total time 'off the firm' might be expected to affect the development of loyalty to individual employers which, it was hoped, decasualization would bring. Dead days were particularly important because they meant the employee concerned lost any chance of earning piecework which, as the next chapter will show, constituted the greater part of a dock worker's weekly earnings.

For time 'off the firm', Firm A and the two departments at the PLA had very different records during Phase 1. At Firm A between twenty and twenty-five per cent of an employee's time was spent 'off the firm'. At the South West India Department of the PLA dockers who worked on the ships spent twelve per cent of their time off the department, while dockers who worked on the quay and in the sheds there spent seven per cent of their time off the department. At the Millwall Department of the PLA, dockers spent about ten per cent of their time off the department.

Dead days were of special significance, as has been said. Estimates from the records of each firm show that Firm A dock workers had one dead day in eight. PLA South West India shipworkers had one dead day in every sixteen while quay workers there averaged only a quarter of a day every seven or eight weeks. From January 1968 PLA Millwall dockers experienced one dead day every six or seven weeks. One reason at least for the difference between Firm A and the PLA was the size of the PLA which helped

[1] NDLB.

individual departments to make arrangements for men who would otherwise have been without work.

Firm B remained outside the Phase 1 scheme since it had provided permanent employment from July 1967. Since then, the firm has not borrowed or loaned dock workers as a matter of policy, but has taken on itself the responsibility for keeping its workers employed. There are no figures of dead days for Firm B, but since the firm has greatly increased the tonnage it handles,[1] the number of dead days is probably low, especially as the agreement obliges the firm to pay its employees the same weekly wage whether there is work or not. For this reason, a dead day did not mean the same thing to an employee at Firm B as it did to dockers elsewhere during Phase 1. For a docker at Firm B it meant no loss of earnings, except for the restricted opportunities for overtime.

During Phase 1 permanent employment was more permanent at Firm B. Because of this difference the remaining chapters on Phase 1 and Phase 2 deal only with the PLA and Firm A, leaving a detailed account of Firm B's experience to Section III.

[1] See below, Chapter 16.

3

Payment Systems

Although Phase 1 brought permanent employment to
dockers, it did not change the piecework payment systems
under which they worked. This chapter will describe these
systems and the use of overtime, to show how the formal
rules which governed them were supplemented by informal
bargaining. The payment system for both the PLA and the
LOTEA members was a combination of timework and
piecework rates. During Phase 1 timework rates were set at
just over £11 per week, but average earnings were between
£30 and £40 per week. Hourly payments for overtime
accounted for just over £2 of the difference between time
rates and actual earnings each week, and the rest was
made up by piecework earnings.

Piecework
The PLA negotiated its piecework rates independently of
other employers, though originally PLA rates were similar
to those of ocean trades employers. PLA rates for imports
were different from their rates for exports.

South West India Department worked the PLA import
rates. The rates were based on commodity and tonnage.
Rates were differentiated according to the goods, and, for
the same goods, according to whether the units handled
were above or below a given weight. Rates also varied
according to the type of packaging. The result was a piecework book of hundreds of rates.

The original piecework rates in 1920 were intended to
yield a surplus of about thirty-three per cent over time

rates. Since then, the time rate rose faster than piecework
rates. When the time rate was increased, a standard adjustment, termed the current percentage increase (or CPI), was
added to the piece rates. Piece rates themselves have not
been altered since the war, and the only change has been
the adjustment of the CPI.[1] The department's figures,
given in Table I, show that these adjustments have failed
to maintain the initial relationship. By 1966 piece rates
had been almost doubled since the war and yet failed to
produce a surplus over time rate earnings. Even if the
initial relationship between piece rates and time rates had
been maintained with thirty-three per cent surplus for
piecework earnings, this would not have sufficed. The time
rate at just over £2 per day was not acceptable to dockers.

TABLE 1

Declining Piecework Surplus of PLA Import Prices
(assuming a constant output)

Date	Day Wage		% Adjust- ment (CPI)	Average Surplus Yielded per hour		Average Surplus
1920	16.0d	(80p)	—	7.9d	(3.3p)	32.9%
1923	10.0d	(50p)	−30%	7.3d	(3p)	48.7%
1941	16.0d	(80p)	—	7.9d	(3.3p)	43.9%
1945	19.0d	(95p)	+ 8%	5.9d	(2.5p)	20.7%
1951	£1.1.0	(£1.05)	+16%	5.5d	(2.3p)	17.5%
1952	£1.2.6	(£1.125)	+22%	5.1d	(2.1p)	15.1%
1953	£1.4.0	(£1.2)	+28%	4.8d	(2p)	13.3%
1955	£1.6.0	(£1.3)	+38.2%	5.11d	(2.1p)	13.1%
1956	£1.8.0	(£1.4)	+48.6%	5.4d	(2.2p)	12.9%
1957	£1.9.6	(£1.475)	+56.56%	5.7d	(2.4p)	12.9%
1958	£1.10.0	(£1.5)	+63.64%	6.0d	(2.5p)	12.9%
1960	£1.12.10	(£1.64)	+69.3%	4.7d	(2p)	9.7%
1962	£1.16.0	(£1.8)	+74.4%	4.1d	(1.7p)	8.0%
1964	£1.17.0	(£1.85)	+74.9%	−1.25d	(−0.5p)	—
1964	£2.1.8	(£2.08)	+83.1%	−4.1d	(−1.7p)	—
1966	£2.4.4	(£2.22)	+92.3%	−5.2d	(−2.2p)	—

Source: Labour Office, South West India Department.

[1] Since the CPI is an across the board percentage increase and since
some commodity rates paid less than others, this method of adjustment of
piecework rates had the effect of making poor rates relatively worse.

Both managers and dockers generally agree that the import piece rates at the South West India Department no longer provided an acceptable level of earnings. Negotiation therefore took place within the department under several heads. Local agreements, i.e formalized regular payments agreed at departmental level and approved by the dock manager, replaced the firm's general rates and applied to all cargo of that type. Examples are rates of 8/0d (40p) for 20 tons of rice and of 7/6d (35p) for 12 tons of rubber. But there were also agreements sanctioned by particular shipping lines for application to their ships only. Thus one line agreed to sanction payment for cargo or packages in units of more than 45 lbs at the rate of 4/6d (22.5p) for 8 tons, and for cargo and packages in units of less than 45 lbs at the rate of 4/6 (22.5p) for 6 tons. Such agreements quickly established a precedent. This particular arrangement subsequently applied to all discharge at that shed. Similarly, sums of money paid on an *ad hoc* basis was sanctioned by particular lines, for example to work a job to a finish in the same day; these also quickly establish a precedent.

More generally, earnings were made up by supplementary payments, either in the form of hourly time rate allowances or *ad hoc* amounts. These were claimed under various headings: by shipworkers for awkwardness of stowage, sorting, and re-stowage, and for delay on the quay or mechanical breakdown; by quay workers for standing by while the ship discharged cargo to barges overside, for excessive sorting in the sheds, or for mechanical failure.[1] Most often payments were made in terms of daywork allowances because disputes centred on the piecework surplus and the effect of making daywork allowances was to increase the surplus by confining piecework earnings to a smaller number of hours. If, for example, two hours daywork was allowed for overside delays in a four-hour period, the piecework surplus was calculated against two

---

[1] For the terminology of the docks, see Appendix I.

hours daywork (not four) and the two hours daywork
was then added. Theoretically at least, these payments
could be distinguished from additional payments made for
exceptionally dirty cargo or for time lost through bad
weather.

In Phase 1, negotiations on each piecework bill took place
between a traffic officer[1] and a representative of a gang.
If there was no agreement at this stage, then the shop
steward was brought in. If there was still no agreement
then the case was argued between the shop steward and the
senior traffic officer. Above this level the dispute might be
taken to the docks manager or to the Group Joint
Committee (composed equally of labour and management
representatives).[2] At both these levels the trade union
full-time officer was usually brought in, but in practice
most disputes were settled before that. One possible reason
is the dissatisfaction with 'Group Joint' expressed by all
the shop stewards interviewed at the South West India
Department.

Since rates played such a small part in determining earnings and there were so many headings under which extra
claims could be made, there was little to guide the bargaining process, and vague and often conflicting criteria appeared to influence the parties. The traffic officer admitted
that his estimation of the price of the job was based on the
rate and what had previously been paid for that type of job.
Gang representatives seemed more concerned with what
was being paid to other gangs, and with subjective estimation of effort expended. A comparison with higher tonnages
achieved by other gangs led one representative to claim
'there must have been hold-ups' on his own job. The
respective capabilities of different gangs were also the subject of comparisons. Managers and trade union officials
agreed on the existence of good gangs and poor gangs,
and gangs had their own estimation of their comparative
worth. Shipworkers in the South West India Department

---

[1] For managerial organization, see Appendix II.
[2] For the structure of negotiating committees, see Appendix III.

continually compared their earnings with those of quay workers, expressing discontent because their earnings did not reflect what they considered to be a higher skill and effort required for shipwork; and managers agreed with them.

In addition, standards were subject to change. It was often pointed out that dockers aimed at some figure for a daily wage—£6, £7, or £8—but the figure was not constant. The reason was not only a change in the general estimation of a fair day's pay, but also variations in the estimation of what was dirty, arduous or even dangerous work, as mechanization increased and general standards rose.

Any commodity piecework system in the docks encourages anomalies. In the absence of clear criteria in the South West India Department each party made a daily relative assessment of jobs, probably on a different basis. The foremen had been completely superseded as first line negotiators and, not surprisingly, traffic officers admitted that they spent an average of four hours a day on negotiations. This limited the amount of time available for their other duties, and one result of this was to reduce their knowledge of the jobs performed which in turn affected their performance in negotiations.

Millwall worked the PLA export rates. Since decasualization the PLA has increased the exports handled by its Millwall Department and diverted the latter's imports elsewhere. Besides increasing the tonnage handled by the department, this policy also levelled out the workload in the department. Before decasualization most weeks had peak days and off days according to the pattern of traffic. Monday and Tuesday were usually 'quiet' days in which ships discharged any imports they had, whereas Thursday and Friday brought peak demands for labour in order to enable ships to sail fully loaded on Friday.

PLA export rates were adjusted, like its import rates, by overall percentage increases rather than by individual adjustments of rates. The CPI for PLA export rates, at

78.04 per cent, was lower than the CPI for import rates. This reflected the fact that piecework earnings were rising more rapidly on exports than on imports because exports were more mechanized. Mechanization of exports also allowed a much simpler classification of cargo so that a general rate applied to most exports. One of the traffic officers said that this rate was expected to yield a surplus of 8/0d (40p) per hour, i.e. 160 per cent surplus on time rates. He contended that there was general acceptance of the rate only so long as it produced this surplus.

But the workload varied from one task to another. Striking[1] was generally harder than quay work since the latter was more mechanized; for the same reason it was said to be easier to achieve a given level of earnings on quay work. There were delays in the flow of work for both tasks. It is difficult to judge whether or not they were a more persistent feature of striking operations, but these caused more consistent claims for extra payments. These payments, like similar payments at the South West India Department, showed how a piecework system, aimed at relating pay to tonnage, leads to payments for time in which work might have been done. Restowage, which here usually involves the movement of cargo within a shed, provides an example. Since it was difficult to measure the tonnage restowed, a 'con'[2] or lump sum payment might be made. Where workers thought this con was insufficient, daywork allowances were paid on the following basis. An estimate was made of the 'standard' tonnage an 'average' gang would shift in an hour with 'normal' effort and without delays.[3] The tonnage cleared was then divided by this standard to yield an acceptable piecework figure for a piecework period. The extra hours actually worked were paid at time rates. Thus payment might be made for restowage which had not actually been carried out. Hence restowage became a head-

---

[1] Striking is unloading from road or rail transport for export.

[2] 'Con' here means condition payment.

[3] The inverted commas in this sentence are around issues which might prove contentious.

ing for payments made to 'bump up' earnings which might be low for other reasons such as the weight of the cargo.

The payment system at the Millwall Department gave rise to less obvious signs of continual friction than at South West India. Traffic officers said that they spent only half an hour a day on negotiations. One reason often suggested was that the level of tonnage and therefore of earnings[1] was more consistent and higher at the Millwall Department. However earnings figures at Millwall are neither higher nor more stable than at the South West India Department. The difference might be explained by the relative formality and simplicity of the payment system at the Millwall Department which provided less ground for argument. An example of this was the platform below which workers would not allow their earnings to fall. While the platform was roughly the same in both departments, it was achieved by different means. For the South West India Department, earnings were built up to this level by continual negotiation over delays, awkward cargoes, etc., whereas there has been a Departmental minimum guarantee at Millwall for seven years. Over the period from 1962 to 1969 this was increased from 2/6d (12.5p) to 6/0d (30p) per hour above time rates.

In addition, there was a series of minimum tonnage guarantees for imports at the Millwall Department to cope with delays: when a ship's gang was moved from hold to hold, the quay gang servicing it was allowed ten per cent extra tonnage for each separate 'purchase', i.e. ship's gear used; for delay due to discharge 'overside' a ten per cent increase on actual tonnage was allowed for every three hours of overside, and a twenty per cent increase on actual tonnage for every four hours of overside. But as has been stated before, not much import work was done in the Millwall Department.

Firm A had a similar piecework system to the PLA, but, since the firm is a member of the LOTEA its piece rates

[1] See Chapter 4.

were those of the Ocean Shipowners Group Joint
Committee. These were even more complex than the PLA
rates. For loading and discharging there were more than
5,000 rates. A further complication was the use of measurement as well as deadweight tonnage for loading miscel-
laneous general cargo. Forty cubic feet was considered a
'measurement' ton. Up to a maximum of nine tons, payment was related to the measurement tonnage or three
times the deadweight tonnage whichever was the greater;
over nine tons it was related to the measurement tonnage
or three times the deadweight tonnage, whichever was less.[1]
For example:

Deadweight Tonnage	Measurement Tonnage	Tonnage paid
1 ton	10 tons	9 tons
10 tons	32 tons	30 tons
50 tons	32 tons	32 tons

Although there had been no general alteration in rates
since 1956, individual rates were changed or marked up.
These changes occurred either as a result of the recommendation of a viewing committee of the Ocean Trade Group
Joint Committee on a new cargo, commodity or method
of handling, or when rates were considered to be badly
out of line. Then they could be changed by the Joint
Committee's sub-committee on piecework rates on a request
from the union officials sitting on this sub-committee. There
was also provision for a disputed job to be viewed by a
representative committee of the Joint Committee, but
neither side at Firm A took discussion beyond the shop
steward or union official.[2] No one at Firm A remembered
seeing a committee of the OTGJC for years.[3] The Joint

[1] Firm A's earnings figures do not indicate that this arrangement had
much effect in levelling earnings (see Chapter 4).

[2] Firm A's workers are mainly NASDU members and this union has an
'outdoor' officer who spends most of his time in Millwall and India Dock.

[3] The experience of Firm A differed from that of those stevedores who
worked for shipping companies which demanded the formal approval of
the OTGJC before sanctioning additional payments.

Committee rates were intended to yield about £4 for an 8 hour day in 1969 but in fact daily earnings were averaging about £6 to £9. It follows that additions were being made by informal bargaining as at the PLA. The superintendents admitted that a great proportion of their time was spent on negotiation. There were complaints about good jobs and bad jobs. Arguments arose over jobs involving bad stowage, narrow working space, or spilt cargo. As in the PLA, lump payments or time allowances were negotiated in compensation. One shipping line which had experienced delays caused by negotiations had sanctioned the payment by Firm A of a flat rate to replace the piecework rates.

In all three areas, the two PLA departments and Firm A, different degrees of complexity and informality were noticed in the payment systems used. But in all three formal rates were being supplemented by *ad hoc* negotiations and informal settlements.

Overtime

Overtime was another important component of the earnings achieved at the PLA and Firm A, and it was subject to negotiations like those which characterized piecework. It is scarcely any exaggeration to say that the normal working day was 8 a.m. to 7 p.m.[1] How far this overtime was actually worked varied according to the dockers' control over their pace of work on a particular job. Striking was a job where overtime was said to be worked, whereas work on board ship and on the quay often finished earlier than 7 p.m. One reason for the difference is that dockers have no control of the flow of traffic when striking; moreover, if it is correct that it was harder to achieve a given level of tonnage and earnings at the Millwall Department on striking than on quay work, then more overtime work might be expected on striking. By contrast dockers working a hold

---

[1] Dockers in London worked an average 6 hours overtime a week in 1968, slightly more even than in Liverpool (NDLB figures).

on a ship were able to increase the pace of work once
overtime orders were given so as to be finished by 5 p.m.
or even earlier, and still be paid for overtime. There had
been conflict over the timing of overtime orders; generally
orders for 7 p.m. working were given by 1.00 p.m., though
sometimes later at the South West India Department.[1]

In many cases, then, overtime represented units of payment rather than extra hours worked. Conflict over whether
overtime orders should be given was therefore similar to
friction about other supplementary payments. The argument was about the price of a job rather than over the time
it should take. A two hour stoppage at Firm A illustrated
this. One of several gangs aboard a ship was refused overtime orders. By common consent it had done good work
the previous day. Consequently in management's opinion,
there was insufficient tonnage in its hold to warrant 7 p.m.
orders. Given what the gang had done in the morning, the
manager felt the job should be finished before 4.00 p.m.
The gang argued: (a) that it was being penalized for its
good work during the previous day; (b) that all other
gangs were on 7 p.m. working; (c) even if the manager
was right about when the job should finish, 7 p.m. orders
were given for many other jobs which finished just as early;
(d) that working conditions were excessively cold (it was a
refrigerated hold) and working was difficult because the
cartons had frozen. These arguments were similar to those
that accompanied piecework negotiations. Overtime was
subject to the same negotiating pressures as piecework.

Comparative Pressures and Management Response
The operation of piecework and overtime in the two
firms revealed pressures for earnings greater than those
provided by the formal systems of pay. There were at least
three sources of pressure for higher earnings. Dockers
compared their earnings with what they had previously
earned on other jobs, and often found them wanting.

[1] The minimum period of weekday overtime was a single unit of two
hours from 5 to 7 p.m.

They sought a consistency and security of earnings that piecework did not give them. They also compared their own earnings with those of other dockers, and often found that the differences in the skill or effort of different gangs (or the similar skill or effort of similar gangs) went unrecognized. They sought a wage structure which piecework did not give them. They were also trying to increase their total earnings at a time when the prices and incomes policy constrained formal collective bargaining. All three sources of pressure could combine in actual negotiations.

The pressures were complicated, and at times even contradictory. Management claimed they were irresponsible, but management's response was scarcely more consistent. For example, managers accepted that inflationary pressures on piecework prices had been understandable under the casual system. They felt men were justified in exploiting their earnings opportunities because there was no guarantee that work would be available the next day. After decasualization managers argued that continued pressure threatened the viability of the port. However, employment was already contracting because of technological and commercial changes. The argument that high wages would drive firms out of existence could not be expected to restrain pay demands when it was the lowest paying sectors of the London docks (the London and St Katharine docks and the Surrey and Commercial docks) which had gone out of business and when private wharfingers were closing their operations because of the value of their sites for different purposes.

The formal piecework system defined the employers' view of the proper relationship between reward and effort, although they had other considerations in mind, such as the differential profit from various cargoes which could mean that some cargoes paid better than others. However, other variables in dock work, such as the weather, machines, delays due to the loading of barges or restowing, could produce different outputs and different rewards for a given effort. Thus employers retreated to a swings and roundabouts philosophy. By this they meant that since work in the docks was variable and conditions uncontrollable, workers should accept the bad jobs with the good without complaint. Thus the employers admitted that the system was inequitable.

A major review of the piecework systems was discouraged by the government's prices and incomes policy and by negotiations on new methods of pay in Phase 2. Such a review, if it increased earnings, might not meet the government's criteria for pay increases. Also it was the intention of the Phase 2 negotiators to move away from piecework. A review of piecework, which dockers accepted, would have been likely to delay the introduction of Phase 2. Accordingly, the formal criteria of the piecework system were necessarily supplemented by other criteria, and these were informally and hence haphazardly applied. The resulting confusion multiplied conflicts and disputes. In these disputes the dockers sometimes displayed conflicting values but they were no more inconsistent and illogical than managers switching from belief in a fair reward for effort to the swings and roundabouts argument.

Whatever their arguments, employers, in fact, met pay demands or resisted them according to their ability to pass on increased costs to their customers. The PLA and stevedores seemed to be able to pass on increased costs. Tonnage rates to customers were based on the various schedules of piecework rates operative in London. But as piecework rates became out of date and were supplemented by extra payments, these extra payments were also passed on to customers. Some foreign shippers would demand the formal approval of official arbitration committees before sanctioning extra payments, but most companies had agents at the docks who would agree the payments with the port employers. This system appeared to be acceptable to most shipping companies. Although costs must have risen considerably during Phase 1 (and the PLA for example raised their rates on goods five times between 1967 and 1970) annual tonnages handled by the port remained constant.[1] Labour charges are only one of many costs for shippers. Others include harbour, port, and river dues, and discharging rates. Time lost in port was generally considered more expensive than *ad hoc* settlements.[2] Shipping companies showed more concern to secure a firm and a labour force used to dealing with their type of cargo than with the increase in costs. Even before decasualization, contracting employers worked regularly in certain areas on specialized services. For the same reason the work of shipping companies was not offered on tender to the lowest bidder. There was little evidence of competition between employers in London.

In general, therefore, port employers were able to pass on dockers' pay increases in increased charges to their customers. Of course, they were not always able to do so; nor were they always able to pass on the full increases. Hence they might be inclined to resist some demands, albeit inconsistently. It also became apparent to employers during Phase 1 that this situation of wage and cost drift could not go on indefinitely. This was one reason for seeking a change from conventional piecework to a different pay system in Phase 2.

[1] See *Annual Reports* of the PLA.
[2] The Rochdale report estimated that cargo handling constituted 25 per cent of a typical ship's total costs, and that it spent 60 per cent of its time in port. (*Report of the Committee of Inquiry into Shipping*, 1970, Cmnd. 4337, p. 103).

B

4

Earnings

It is clear from the previous chapter that by 1969 payment systems in the London docks were highly fragmented and informal. The pressures on these systems may be identified from figures and graphs of the movement of earnings in London in general, and in the PLA and Firm A in particular. The origins of pressures from the workers were three-fold. Firstly, a demand that a given effort or willingness to work should be reflected in a given earnings level. This was a demand for security of earnings. Secondly, workers made a comparative judgement of their own worth relative to that of other dockers. This was a wage structure demand. Thirdly, there was a general desire to increase their earnings.

Security of Earnings
The Devlin Committee saw insecurity in the docks as a consequence of casual employment which produced periods of unemployment and caused earnings to fluctuate. The minimum weekly guarantee introduced in 1947 was aimed at alleviating this insecurity. But, as the Committee suggested, this security had little meaning because the fall-back guarantee which put a floor to earnings was below the time rate. In 1967 the fall-back guarantee for London was raised to £17, well above the time rate. But, by an extension of the Committee's argument, the security given by this arrangement and by the regularizing of employment in 1967 was dependent on how far the guaranteed weekly

minimum lay below *average earnings* and how much dockers had to depend upon it. Graph 1 shows that average earnings were well above the guaranteed minimum. Graph 2, giving average earnings for the two selected PLA departments and for all PLA departments in the Millwall and India sector, shows that average earnings for individual firms were also well above the guaranteed £17. Graph 3, showing the weekly movements in earnings of two selected dockers at Firm A, confirms that average earnings were well above the guaranteed minimum which was rarely, if ever, relied upon.

But insecurity is not only a consequence of the size of the drop from average to minimum earnings, but also of the fluctuations in earnings themselves. A minimum *weekly* guarantee did nothing to level out fluctuations in daily or hourly earnings. Graphs 2 and 3 show that average earnings continued to fluctuate violently. This was true both for average earnings within firms, and even more for the earnings of individual dockers.

As has been seen there were demands for departmental daily guarantees in the PLA to smooth out these fluctuations and to raise the minimum *daily* level in earnings. Similarly, the employees of the private stevedores demanded minimum guarantees of £4 10s (£4.50) for the 8 a.m. to 5 p.m. shift and £5 12s (£5.60) for the 8 a.m. to 7 p.m. shift, and got them in August 1969. To increase the security in *hourly* earnings, the daily guarantee was divided by working 'turns': £2 5s (£2.25) for 8 a.m. to 1 p.m.; £3 7s (£3.35) for 1 p.m. to 7 p.m.

Wage Structure

Dockers were concerned with the relationship of their earnings to those of other dockers as well as with security of earnings, and there was no wage structure in the docks to offer different rewards for recognized differences in skill and/or effort. At a general level, dockers at one firm or department were concerned that their earnings did not fall behind those of other firms. As will be seen, Firm B was

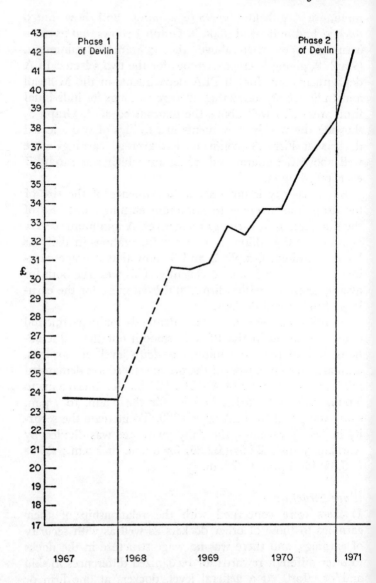

Graph 1   Average Earnings of London Dockers

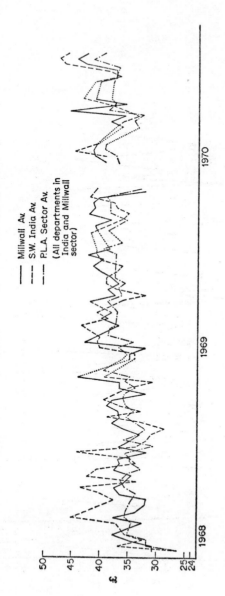

Graph 2   PLA (Millwall and India) Average Earnings

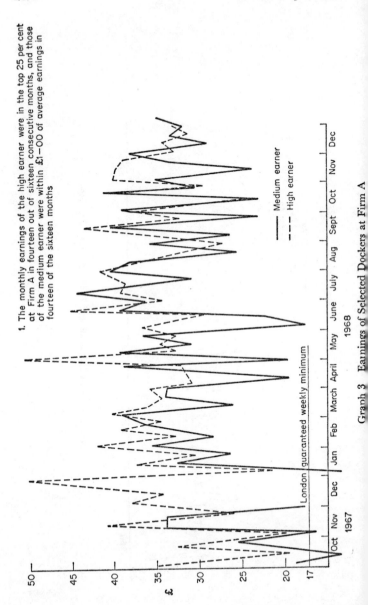

1. The monthly earnings of the high earner were in the top 25 per cent at Firm A in fourteen out of sixteen consecutive months, and those of the medium earner were within £1·00 of average earnings in fourteen of the sixteen months

Graph 3   Earnings of Selected Dockers at Firm A

important as a wage leader and pacesetter in the London docks generally and in the Millwall and India in particular. It is thus interesting to note that average earnings in other firms followed those of Firm B. Graph 4 illustrates this by the comparative movements of cumulative weekly[1] average earnings at Firm B and Firm A.

But dockers were also concerned with the comparisons between their earnings and those of other dockers at the same firm. The graphs show the failure of piecework earnings to reflect accepted differentials in skill or effort. Shipworkers at the PLA South West India Department complained that their earnings were often less than those of quay workers in the same department, despite the greater effort and difficulty involved in shipwork. Graph 5 bears out this complaint. Dockers generally complained that good gangs were not differentiated from poor gangs and might earn less because of the vagaries of piecework. Over a long period of time during which the earning opportunities of the system had equalled out, a good gang might earn more than a poor gang, but a comparison of the weekly earnings of a high and medium earner at Firm A (Graph 3) shows, as the dockers asserted, that this differential could not be relied upon in the short term.

The point can be made in another way. Not only did earnings fluctuate from one firm to another, but there was also a wide spread of earnings from day to day and from week to week within each firm. This spread gave rise to comparative claims of the sort that have been described. To measure it, the standard deviation of all weekly earnings at Firm A was calculated for similar weeks in 1968 and 1970. Next the coefficients of variation were worked out. They showed that the spread was not only constant over the two years but also very large; in fact, twice as large as those normally found for workers in the same grade in pieceworking engineering firms in Coventry where payment systems are known to be chaotic.

[1] The cumulative weekly averages were used to show a general movement in wages by levelling out the fluctuations in weekly earnings at each firm.

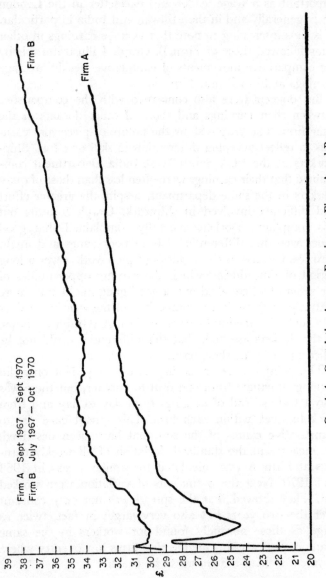

Firm A   Sept 1967 — Sept 1970
Firm B   July 1967 — Oct 1970

Graph 4   Cumulative Average Earnings at Firms A and B

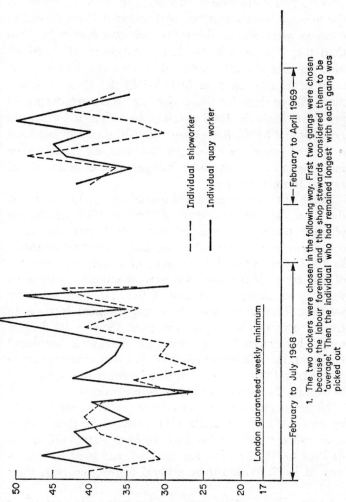

- - - Individual shipworker

——— Individual quay worker

London guaranteed weekly minimum

|← February to July 1968 →| |← February to April 1969 →|

1. The two dockers were chosen in the following way. First two gangs were chosen because the labour foreman and the shop stewards considered them to be 'average'. Then the individual who had remained longest with each gang was picked out

Graph 5   Comparative Earnings of Ship and Quay Workers

Wage Drift[1]

Claims were also aimed at increasing earnings. In this the
dockers had considerable success. The NDLB figures for
the average weekly earnings of London dockers show that
earnings were almost thirty-five per cent higher in 1968
than they had been in the last 37 weeks of 1967. About
nine per cent of this is explained by the modernization payment of 1s (5p) an hour included in the Phase 1 agreement. Wage drift for the period was therefore twenty-six
per cent. Early in 1969 earnings had risen a further six
per cent and by the first quarter of 1970 they had increased
a further twelve per cent. In the next six months they
increased a further six and a half per cent, or at an annual
rate of thirteen per cent.

Some of these increases had special causes. In particular,
the twenty-six per cent drift of 1967 to 1968 can be explained partly by decasualization itself bringing more
continuous employment. Average daily labour requirements
in 1967 were eighty-five per cent of the average number
of workers available. For 1968 average labour requirements
were up to ninety-six per cent of the number of available
workers. Thus there was an average annual increase in
employment of eleven per cent from 1967 to 1968. This
would be expected to produce an increase in earnings.[2]
However, this still leaves much of that year's increase unex-
plained, and there were no further increases in employment
to explain the subsequent increases in earnings.

Under a piecework system, increases in earnings might
be explicable by an increase in tonnage. In fact, annual
total tonnages for London declined from 60.09 million tons
in 1967 to 60.08 million tons in 1968, and to 58.02 million
tons in 1969. Within these general figures, however, there

[1] Wage drift in this study means the increase in average earnings not
accounted for by national and port negotiations between bodies of
employers and the unions.
[2] This increase would not be strictly proportionate to the increase in
employment since unemployed dockers did have a guaranteed fall back
wage.

were weekly and daily fluctuations in trade, and while piecework earnings could be expected to rise as tonnage rose, they did not fall as tonnage fell. This is illustrated by Firm A where tonnage fell five per cent from 1968 to 1969 while the labour costs involved fell only 1.7 per cent.[1]

Wage drift in the docks therefore was not a direct function of higher productivity but apparently—in absence of any other explanation—of the piecework bargaining process. This bargaining was highly informal and subject to different and sometimes conflicting pressures from dockers and employers.

[1] Firm A seems to be typical in this respect. In London as a whole general cargo tonnages (other than fuels) fell by one per cent between 1968 and 1969, while earnings continued to rise.

5

Work Allocation

The previous chapters have shown that, during Phase 1 of Devlin, decasualization did not change the methods of pay or the negotiations associated with them. Equally Phase 1 brought little change, except in detail, in methods of work allocation and the manning of jobs. As before, workers demanded rules or practices that restricted what employers called 'free manning', i.e. their freedom to place or move individuals at will on a given job. The two main restrictions on free manning were the gang system of working and rules on the distribution of work. This chapter will try to explain these two restrictions, and how employers operated within them in allocating work.

Gang Working

The gang system determined the manning of jobs in two ways. Firstly, it sent men to jobs in groups rather than as individuals. The operation of the continuity rule prevented managers breaking up these groups once they were assigned work. Secondly, each job required a separate gang. Thus when cargoes were loaded upon or unloaded from a hatch, received from or delivered to a ship, moved from a shed to transport, and loaded upon or unloaded from transport, each operation had to have its own gang. Employers complained that both aspects of the gang system hampered the most effective use of labour.

But the gang system did not entirely obstruct the flexibility of labour. An individual was not likely to be a permanent member of his gang because 'spare' gangs[1] were

[1] See p. 38 for definition of spare gangs. Other terms are defined in Appendix I.

broken down and absent workers temporarily lost their place in their gangs. Moreover, the size of gangs varied. They had 10–16 members on conventional ships and quays and 3 or 6 on 'mechanized' sheds and quays. However, the main influence on gang size in the sector studied was not the availability of mechanized aids, but the distinction between imports and exports. On exports the PLA had agreed mechanized manning scales with the union prior to decasualization, but after decasualization the negotiations on new manning scales on imports failed to reach agreement even on a shed-by-shed basis. It could be that negotiations on this issue were delayed in view of port negotiations over Phase 2, but the reason given for the failure to extend mechanized manning was the dockers' fear of too rapid a decline in the size of the labour force. PLA managers felt they could have extended their mechanization agreements if their pre-decasualization labour situation had continued. The extra labour they were assigned after decasualization put an end to the possibility of reduced manning.

Employers, however, were ambivalent in their attitude to gang working. While they felt that it led to inefficient use of labour, they also felt that the familiarity of the members of the gang with each other's work improved the performance of men in gangs; and employers supported the gang system by paying the gang as a unit. The only extra payments were those made to specialists such as crane or winch drivers, to gangers, or to machine operators for any time needed to collect and return machines outside normal working hours.

Rules on the distribution of work

The best known restriction was the 'continuity rule' which was central to all the work allocation systems used in Phase 1. The rule operated to retain men who had been assigned to a particular job until it was finished, by reserving jobs for all the gangs originally assigned to them. The details varied according to the type of work and the customs of each firm. Not all jobs were continuity jobs, but shipwork generally was continuity work. Thus when a gang was allocated to a ship it would remain there until the ship was loaded or discharged. Further, the gang would be allocated to a particular hold on a ship and would be 'continuity' to that hold until it was discharged or loaded. Gangs working on the quay would be on continuity work when they were servicing a ship. Although not all jobs were continuity jobs, all work allocation systems were based upon the rule in Phase 1. Firms worked formal or informal rotas whereby gangs were assigned in strict order to continuity jobs and other work was allocated only when these jobs were manned up.

The continuity rule was enforced by the dockers and criticized by the employers because it prevented them from sending the men they wanted to any given job. But it did not originate with the dockers. Although some groups had had individual continuity arrangements prior to the Second World War, the port-wide continuity rule was introduced at the insistence of employers. With a wartime shortage of labour, employers were worried by the practice of the 'best' men choosing only the best-paying jobs and working only the best-paying parts of these jobs. The continuity rule is thus an example of a rule initiated by employers but later maintained as custom and practice by the workers in the face of employer opposition.

Although it was associated with the casual system of work, the continuity rule survived decasualization, but adjustments had to be negotiated to deal with the borrowing and lending of labour under Phase 1. It was a misunderstanding of, or disagreement with, these adjustments that caused the 1967 dock strike in London which cost a quarter of a million working days and, if nothing else, showed the continuing concern of dockers with maintaining the rule. There was a danger that a firm that had borrowed men might then find that it had not enough work for its own permanent men, or, alternatively, that a lending firm might find that it did not have enough men to do its own work. To avoid this, the continuity of a borrowed worker on a continuity job could be broken: (a) if his own employer required him back; or (b) if his temporary employer no longer required him. In practice, work allocation was already so complicated and the labour officers under such pressure from other sources, that borrowed men often were not pulled out of continuity jobs when these circumstances applied.

The continuity rule could be said to deal with the 'ownership' of jobs, and the rotation of gangs around continuity jobs distributed work in a way that was acceptable to dockers. The rule was supplemented by other rules aimed at determining job 'ownership' and at spreading work fairly. For example the 'purchase rule', a rule applying throughout London, governed the division of work within a ship's hold. It dealt with the use of purchase (ships' cranes and winches) in a hold where there were two purchases and two gangs. It stated that in the event of a second gang being brought in to work the hold, the first gang was to use the same purchase as previously. This had the result of dividing the stowage between the two gangs. Where the rule did not apply, there were various informal rules governing the division of cargo in a hold. In the PLA South West India Department an imaginary line was drawn dividing the cargo between forward and aft; the second gang went aft. When any part of the work was finished, forward or aft, the aft gang was 'paid off'. The second gang left and the first gang finished the hold. This arrangement did not apply at Firm A where each gang was 'discharged'[1] as it finished its section of the stowage.

Labour Allocation
During Phase 1, employers, working within the constraints of the gang system and the continuity rule, allocated men to jobs in rotation. Large firms like the PLA favoured

---

[1] 'Paid off' and 'discharged' were the terms used by participants. They are terms clearly applicable to the casual system but are carried over, like the rules themselves, to a system of permanent employment.

formal rotas, while smaller firms like Firm A favoured informal rotas. Whether the rotas were formal or informal, labour departments would first 'man up' continuity jobs in a set order from a list of gangs. This list of gangs was ordered according to how recently they had been on continuity work. Those who had been on such work most recently were at the end of the list. Only when all continuity jobs were allocated was it possible to split up a gang. The gangs left over were 'spare' and would be split to fill up the complement of other gangs. Gangs were split in order, though here the order was reversed because fairness demanded that gangs which had most recently come off continuity work should be the first to be split up although they were at the end of the rota.

This system depended on lists of gangs on continuity work or non-continuity work, of gangs most recently split up, of individuals most recently 'off the firm' (lent to another employer) or most recently 'missing' (separated from) his gang. The task of the labour department was not to man jobs as effectively as possible but rather to ensure that the different jobs and work opportunities in a firm or department were distributed among its different gangs.

Management rarely tried to cost these practices or to specify alternative methods of working. Indeed where managers felt that an assignment would improve the men's acquaintance with the daily flow of traffic and so increase their efficiency, they would occasionally assign men to particular jobs for a week even when they were not required to do so by the continuity rule. Most employers favoured some form of gang working. What they wanted was greater power to break down or split up gangs on the job.

The restrictions on 'free manning' had repercussions on the system of payment. Particular work or cargoes could be identified as separate jobs because they had separate piecework prices. The continuity and other rules assigned these jobs to particular gangs. Thus on quay work, cargo for export 'belonged' to the striking gang which unloaded from the transport bringing it to the docks, and to the quay gang that delivered it from the shed to the ship's side. This arrangement was upset, however, when the cargo was delivered direct to the ship from the transport, either because it was hazardous, or frozen, or (more recently) because it was packed in containers. According to the original piecework agreements, these gangs should be paid only the time rate for the period they stood by while such cargo was delivered. But in one of the firms studied there had been a successful demand from the striking and quay gangs for an additional payment for such direct cargoes on the grounds that piecework would have been paid if the cargoes had gone through the sheds as usual.

Rationale for Work Rules and Practices

To employers these rules and practices were restrictive while to dock workers they were protective. Dockers justi- fied them because they spread work to offer employment to as many employees as possible and because they shared work opportunities fairly. These justifications originated with the casual system but fears of unemployment and under-employment remained after 1967. Phase 1 saw the closure of three of the six sectors of the London docks and of many of the port's private wharfingers, including the largest. There was a decline by twenty-five per cent in the number of registered dock workers in London between 1967 and 1969.[1] The fear of an imposed contraction in the size of the labour force was evident in the 'no redun- dancy' pledge won from employers in 1967. Statutory redundancy payments had no application in dock work because of the previous casual nature of employment there. The decline in the size of the labour force that occurred during Phase 1 was achieved under a voluntary severance scheme. The men offered themselves for early retirement and were compensated according to their number of years in the docks.

[1] Annual Reports of NDLB.

In addition to unemployment, under-employment remained a feature of dock work. Firms differed in their ability to provide continuous work for their newly permanent workers. Even full-employed dockers experienced delays in working between jobs, and piecework penalized workers for periods they were out of work or delayed.

Piecework also continued to create good and bad jobs. There was thus scope for favouritism and the dockers suspected that employers might continue to practise it after decasualization as they were believed to have done under the casual system. Dockers therefore maintained their rules on the distribution of work during Phase 1.

The Devlin Committee had suggested that restrictive work practices would have to cease if dock work was to become efficient and the cost of decasualization met. But the Committee appreciated that they could only be removed by negotiations which would also involve changes in payment systems. During Phase 1 piecework continued as before and the system of work allocation also remained unchanged.

6

Strikes

The high propensity to strike in the docks was one of the reasons for the setting up of the Devlin Committee, and one criterion of success for any changes recommended by the Committee will be a diminution in the incidence of strikes. The Devlin Committee confirmed the belief that the docks were strike-prone, and presented the following table (Table II) in their final report.

TABLE II

Strikes in the Docks 1930–64

Industry	Average number of man-days lost yearly in disputes per thousand workers		
	1930/38	1947/55	1956/64
Docks	285	3,134	1,091
Shipbuilding & Repair	325	890	2,349
Coalmining	1,034	778	627
Engineering & Vehicles	80	162	411
Construction	60	69	110
Textiles	1,311	22	30
Food, drink, tobacco	10	15	27

Source: Final Report of the Devlin Committee.

The Devlin Committee's recommendations on decasualization and on changes in payment systems, work methods, and union and employer structure were intended to reduce the incidence of strikes, but at least until all their recommendations have been put into effect it would be unfair to judge the Committee a 'failure' because the incidence of strikes remains high. By 1971 Phase 2 of Devlin was in

operation in only three of Britain's major ports. But Phase 1
was put into effect nationally in 1967, and the strike record
of the docks since then will show whether permanent
employment, by itself, had any effect on the propensity to
strike.

Table III shows that the docks have remained a strike-
prone industry. Until the end of 1969 decasualization
had not reduced strikes. But these figures are national.
Table IV, drawn from NDLB figures, shows that there are
considerable differences between ports. This table shows
that since decasualization, London has been relatively
strike-free and Liverpool has been strike-prone. There is no

TABLE III

Strikes in the Docks 1967–69

Industry	Average number of man-days lost yearly per 1000 employees			
	1967	1968	1969	1967/69
Docks	4,450	850	3,500	2,933
Shipbuilding & Repairs	750	1,800	1,000	1,183
Coalmining	225	125	2,700	1,013
Motor vehicles	1,000	1,800	3,100	1,967
Construction	125	150	175	150
All industries	125	200	300	175

Source: D.E.P. Gazette.

TABLE IV

Strike Records of Different Ports, 1967–69

Year		No. of Strikes	Man-days lost	Days lost per man annually
1967	Nationally	172	571,578	10
	Liverpool	28	288,798	24
	London	31	252,126	11
1968	Nationally	284	74,439	1·5
	Liverpool	80	39,042	3·25
	London	50	12,793	0·5
1969	Nationally	376	242,220	4·75
	Liverpool	97	100,290	8·6
	London	33	43,346	2·2

Source: NDLB.

reason to believe this is a particularly new situation for London however; as Table V shows London's strike record has not changed since 1964. Consequently, if London is relatively strike-free, decasualization is not the cause.

TABLE V

Strikes per year in London

Year	No. of strikes	Total Man-days lost	Man-days lost per registered dock worker
1964	46	30,921	1·2
1965	22	4,592	0·3
1966	25	31,840	1·3
1967	31	252,126	11·0
1968	50	12,793	0·5

Source: NDLB.

Beyond provoking a massive strike in 1967 in London and Liverpool, decasualization *itself* does not appear to have altered the strike propensity and pattern for the industry in general nor for London in particular. Equally, there is no evidence that the causes of strikes changed with decasualization. This can be shown two ways. Firstly, the DE gives a breakdown of the causes of days lost in strikes by industry group. Table VI shows, for a year before

TABLE VI

Causes of Stoppages in Transport and Communication

	1969 *Total Man-Days lost*	1966 *Total Man-Days lost*
Wage claims	565,000	890,000
Other wage claims	40,000	13,000
All wage disputes	605,000	903,000
Hours of work	1,000	2,000
Demarcation disputes	24,000	50,000
Disputes about employment or discharge of workers	10,000	33,000
Personnel questions	5,000	3,000
Other working arrangements, rules and discipline	33,000	57,000
Trade Union status	26,000	15,000
Sympathetic action	75,000	8,000
Total	779,000	1,071,000

Source: DE Gazette.

decasualization and a year afterwards, the breakdown for transport and communications, which includes the docks. Wage claims and disputes dominate the table in both years. In 1966 they constituted ninety per cent while in 1969 eighty per cent of the time lost. The major reason for the drop was an increase in sympathetic action. If anything, this indicates a widening of the area affected by any strike rather than a new cause.

TABLE VII

Causes of Stoppage at the PLA (Millwall and India) 1967–70

	Millwall	S.W. India	South Quay	North Quay	All Depts.	Total
Wages	5	9	8	14	1	37
Hours of work		3				3
Demarcation disputes						
Redundancy, dismissal						
Trade Union recognition and status						
Closed shop						
Working arrangements rules and discipline	4	5	1	5	2	17
Sympathetic strike						
*Political strikes					4	4
Total	9	17	9	19	7	61

Source: PLA (Millwall and India Dock Office).

* These refer to strikes against government bills on immigration, industrial relations, and port nationalization.

A closer analysis of the causes of strikes is possible by looking at the data provided by the PLA for all stoppages at all its departments in the India and Millwall sector. These, broken down by cause, are given in Table VII. This table shows a pattern of the causes of strikes similar to that revealed in DE figures. The majority of days in the DE analysis were lost in wage disputes and the majority of stoppages in the PLA were about wages. Indeed, under Phase 1, almost all strikes at the PLA (Millwall and India) were either about wages under piecework or about questions of working arrangements and rules. The previous chapter showed that working arrangements were strongly influenced by piecework, so piecework was connected directly or indirectly with most disputes. This may explain why the great majority of disputes had a limited coverage. Only four out of sixty-one strikes affected all departments, and the average number of men involved in a dispute in 1968 and 1969 at the PLA (India and Millwall) was 130 and 91 respectively. Perhaps for the same reasons, strikes were short-lived, lasting an average of 6½ hours in each of those years. But there was a tendency for strikes to get larger and longer in 1970, even before the national strike in July;[1] on the average they involved 312 men and lasted 8 hours in the first six months of 1970.

The departmental breakdown in Table VII shows that strikes occurred more frequently at the import departments of South West India and North Quay. Work here was less mechanized and delays more frequent than on exports. Official piecework rates were less applicable and negotiations for supplementary payments were longer and more frequent. Labour costs were higher for the PLA on imports than exports so that greater resistance might be expected to wage demands on imports. Further, the department with most strikes, North Quay, was both the lowest paying and the least profitable department in the sector.

Piecework was therefore central to virtually all the strikes experienced by the PLA from October 1967 to June 1970, and can explain the different strike records of the several departments. Firm A has no data on strikes but investigations there did not suggest that its strike pattern and incidence were dissimilar to those of the PLA.

Previous chapters have shown that the payment systems and work practices, developed when employment was casual in the London docks, survived decasualization. Not surprisingly the chapter has shown that the pattern and incidence of industrial disputes did not change during Phase 1.

---

[1] No explanation is given for the tendency for strikes to become longer in 1970 beyond saying that this was part of a national trend in the first half of that year.

7

Phase 2 Negotiations

So far it has been shown how decasualization was put into practice in London after September 1967; how pay and work methods were determined in London during Phase 1; how piecework gave rise to inflationary pressures and underpinned the dockers' rules on manning and methods of work which were considered restrictive by employers; and how piecework gave rise to the same pattern of strikes in London after decasualization as before.

Employers were generally aware during Phase 1 that their payment systems were having these detrimental effects, so there was some pressure to move to a new system of pay with Phase 2. Nevertheless not all of them relished the move away from the incentive pay systems. Contracting stevedore employers, in particular, felt incentives were necessary to maintain productivity in the port. They had not changed their methods of day-to-day supervision and not all of them felt able to do so. Unilateral worker control of the pace and methods of work appeared to suit them. Other employers who had invested in containerization and other forms of mechanized handling were more aware of the deficiencies of piecework and keener to change their methods of pay and work allocation. The PLA is an obvious example here with its considerable investment in new berths for container traffic at Tilbury. Some employers were already negotiating terminal agreements on new pay systems in 1967. However, the main lay committee of the TGWU dockers in London, Number One Docks Group, imposed a ban in January 1968 on further local agreements on mechanization until Phase 2 was negotiated for the port generally. Thus port employers and shipping companies with heavy capital commitments in new methods of work were forced to negotiate for these on a port-side basis.

This division of interest among employers can be shown by a chronology of negotiations on Phase 2 in London.

November 1968: The employers unsuccessfully demanded the removal of the container ban and the LOTEA offered £21 5s (£21.25) plus a bonus reported to be fifty per cent. In return they wanted shiftwork and the removal of restrictive practices. The unions wanted a higher basic than this plus a bonus.

January 1969: The PLA offered an alternative of £29 plus a smaller bonus to give in total a similar weekly wage to that of the LOTEA's offer. The TGWU rejected the possibility of two different basic wages.

March 1969: The unions were reported to be pressing other employers to offer the same as the PLA and employers were reported to be considering £27 for light duty men, £29 for quay workers and £31 for shipworkers. Figures on earnings had been published showing average earnings to be £31 per week. On 27 March the unions asked for a basic wage of £35 plus a bonus which was negotiable.

April 1969: The employers offered £24 for light duty men, £32 10s (£32.50) for quay workers and £34 for shipworkers; the offers for quay and shipworkers included a £3 10s (£3.50) bonus element. The chairman of the LOTEA, who was leading the employers' side in the negotiations, spelt out six conditions attaching to this offer:

(i) Acceptance of shift work.
(ii) A working week of 33¾ hours.
(iii) Weekend working if required.
(iv) Full flexibility and mobility. This, he said, had to be complete—by which was meant that the workers could, in the first instance, be deployed at the employer's discre-

tion. If anyone felt aggrieved he was to appeal through normal grievance procedures.

(v) Complete observance by men of the agreement. If any man or gang was found not to be complying with the agreement, then there should be a 'cooling off' period of 4 hours, during which time the men would be required to resume normal working. If they did not, payment would be stopped.

(vi) Employers insisted on a 'balanced labour force' by which they meant getting rid of those unfit for dock work.

May 1969: This offer was considered and finally turned down by a joint committee of lay members of the TGWU and NASDU. The committee informed the employers that future negotiations should proceed on the basis of the claim of a £35 basic for a 35 hour week with shift work.

June 1969: A major firm operating outside the port scheme, Firm B in this study, signed its second agreement with the TGWU. This gave men £39 for a 35 hour week less meal breaks, and introduced shiftwork. The agreement was reported as a patternmaker for the rest of the port.

September 1969: After several months without progress the TGWU raised its demand to £28 for light duty men and £37 10s (£37.50) for ship and quay workers plus a five per cent productivity bonus for a 30 hour week worked on a shift basis.

The chairman of the LOTEA guardedly denied that he had forecast a thirty-three per cent drop in productivity when piecework was abolished. But, he added, 'it is clear that in a situation where there is not going to be piecework with people nearly killing themselves to boost their earnings —there could be a decline in output . . . thirty-three per cent would be unacceptable'.[1]

The employers offered £25 for light duty and £33 10s (£33.50) for the rest, with a 10s (50p) a day differential for shipwork and similar additional shift payments for gangers and crane drivers, all for a 31 hour week worked

[1] *The Port*, 25 September 1969.

on a shift basis. These figures were said to incorporate a bonus element and any offer of a separate bonus must involve a lowering of the time rates. They said this was their final offer.

November 1969: TGWU members turned down the employers' offer in a mass ballot.

February 1970: The employers offered £30, plus bonuses based on standard target performances equivalent to 150 tons of bag work per shift for a standard bonus of £7 6s 5d (£7.32) a week. Further bonuses would be paid on a scale according to how men exceeded standard targets; the standard target was considered attainable by current piecework effort. TGWU officials were reported to be sceptical about the 'revival of piecework in another form' because of the delays and abnormalities associated with piecework which led to failures to reach accepted tonnages. TGWU lay committees rejected these 'piecework proposals'.

On 26 February employers offered £37 for shipwork, £34 10s (£34.50) for quay work, and £26 for light duty men. Lay delegates of the TGWU recommended acceptance of this offer and in another ballot in March it was accepted. The settlement was subsequently delayed and the figures raised by the national dock strike in July 1970 and the Pearson Report that followed it. Phase 2 began in September 1970 with £39 for shipwork, £36 10s (£36.50) for quay work, and £28 for light duty men.

What do these negotiations show? Generally, the long delay before starting the Phase 2 negotiations (over a year after Phase 1 began) and the length of time they took may indicate that some employers were not greatly enamoured with what Phase 2 seemed likely to bring. The very different offers originally made by the LOTEA and the PLA reflect differing opinions as to what Phase 2 should accomplish. Throughout the negotiations, the contracting stevedores—through the LOTEA—reiterated a preference for retaining an incentive element and were dubious of their ability to maintain (and they talked of maintaining rather than of increasing) their throughput without incen-

tive payments. Evidence of this is found in the LOTEA's
initial offer, their chairman's statement in September 1969
on the expected drop in productivity, and their penulti-
mate offer in February 1970. The PLA from the start
was thinking of a high fixed wage. As the next chapter
shows, the Phase 2 agreement marked a compromise
between the two positions.

The difference between the PLA and the stevedores may
reflect the division between ship and quay work. Quay
work requires less manual effort and skill than shipwork
and, being more mechanized, is more consistent in work
content. Under Phase 1, it appeared subject to fewer
restrictive practices and greater management control. Stevedores employing predominantly ship labour, and the PLA
employing predominantly quay labour, might therefore be
expected to differ over the consequences of abandoning
piecework.

Why then did the stevedores agree to the deal? They
gave every impression of being forced to accept it because
of the increasing impatience of dockers, and because of the
pressure from the shippers and other port employers whose
investment in mechanization was threatened by the
container ban. In addition, their conduct in the negotiations marks out the LOTEA as particularly lacking in
initiative. As the majority party on the employers' side they
failed to move on Phase 2 and the container ban until
Overseas Containers Limited were ready to start their new
Australian container service to Tilbury; they failed to settle
before the second agreement of Firm B whose date, terms,
and effects were clearly foreseeable. It was not until April
1969 that they spelt out what was required by way of flexibility and mobility of labour. When they did, their terms of
absolute employer discretion seemed to reflect questionable
thinking on the nature of collective bargaining; and more
significantly, the terms appeared to be impractical in face
of the worker-controlled pace and methods of work under
piecework.

8

The Phase 2 Agreement

The previous section described the influence of piecework on job regulation in London under Phase 1. Rules on payment were imprecise, often informal and subject to conflicting pressures. Piecework also influenced the rules on the distribution of work and the mobility of labour. Supervision was minimal and the pace of work was determined by the workers. From the dockers' point of view the rules they imposed were essential to satisfy their norms of fairness and security, but for management they were the cause of inefficient use of labour, a high rate of wage drift, and a high propensity to strike. It was to solve these problems and to implement the other recommendations of the Devlin Committee that Phase 2 was negotiated for London and put into operation in September 1970.

The Terms of the Agreement
The Phase 2 agreement is contained in what dockers and employers call the Green Book. The Green Book's stated aims are to promote efficiency, to facilitate mechanization and to bring progressive improvement of the wage structure and conditions of employment. It recognizes that problems can only be solved by negotiation between trade union representatives and management.

It prescribes a working week of 35 hours, less $3\frac{3}{4}$ hours for meals, to be worked in two shifts (7 a.m.–2 p.m., and 2 p.m.–9 p.m.). All travelling, washing and changing is to take place outside of working hours. Shifts are to rotate weekly but management can vary this arrangement so long

51

as the maximum continuous period on the afternoon shift is one week. Overtime is voluntary and worked on a rota within each firm. It is restricted to single shift working on weekends and bank holidays; 8 a.m.–noon on Saturdays, and 8 a.m.–3 p.m. on Sundays and bank holidays. Employees are to be notified of weekend working at the latest on the Friday.

The wage structure divides the labour force into two: Category A, fit to undertake cargo handling; and Category B, unfit for cargo handling. Category A men are paid £36.50 a week. In addition they receive 50p a shift when working as part of a ship's gang or as a ganger, 60p a shift when driving a crane, and 25p a shift when handling frozen cargo. Category B men are paid £28 a week. All overtime shifts are paid at double the basic rate: £8.34 for the four hour Saturday shift and £14.60 for the seven hour Sunday and bank holiday shift for Category A, and £6.40 and £11.20 for Category B. But there is a single rate for holiday pay and sick pay. Movement between categories is subject to medical examination, with the National Dock Labour Board as the final arbiter.

There are deductions for poor time keeping. A fifth of the basic weekly wage is deducted for a day's absence with lesser deductions for shorter periods. Schedule 1 provides contingency payments for individuals collecting gear, unlocking sheds, etc., before or after a shift to ensure that full use is made of the shift.

The agreement requires dockers to observe certain work practices. Firstly, dockers must accept overnight/pre-shift orders to report as directed. Secondly, they must give complete mobility and flexibility as required by the employer including:

   (i) movement of employees or gangs to other work on either ship or quay at any time within a shift, including ship to quay and quay to ship;

   (ii) movement of employees or gangs from discharging to loading and vice versa at any time within a shift;

(iii) commencement and continuation of work irrespective of the number of men employed unless the employer deems this impracticable in which case men will be redeployed;

(iv) adjustment in the strength of shed or area crews when required by the employer with employees being transferred to sheds as required within and between an area; and

(v) an acceptance of any duties which the man is competent to perform.

Thirdly, the employer has the right to place men in jobs at his discretion but an employee who wishes to query a specific instance of the exercise of this discretion in which he has been personally concerned may do so through the grievance procedures.[1] Fourthly, dockers are also required to achieve a satisfactory level of output. If an employer feels an employee is failing in this he is to consult the employee's representatives. After that there is provision for a special arbitration committee in each sector to review the case on request from either party. If a docker does not comply with the arbitration decision, he is no longer entitled to pay and is subject to the disciplinary proceedings of the Dock Workers' Employment Scheme 1967. A docker who regularly fails to work at the accepted speed is subject to the same disciplinary provisions. Refusal or failure by dockers to carry out their obligations under this agreement is regarded as a stoppage of work. No payment is to be made and the employer may redirect other men to do the job or put in replacements.

A schedule of the agreement sets out the credentials and election procedure for shop stewards and their rights and functions, with provision for full-time or 'duty' shop stewards. Ocean Trades employers are to engage one or more according to the size of the firm, and all Ocean Trades shop stewards were to be duty stewards for the first

---

[1] The existing grievance procedures for the Ocean Trades and the PLA which were intended for piecework disputes are set out in the agreement as appropriate for such complaints.

two months, with provision for extending the period by mutual agreement of the Enclosed Docks Modernization Committee. There is no provision for duty shop stewards in the PLA, but an appropriate number of shop stewards is to be released full-time at the Authority's discretion 'for a special period' to enable important matters to be dealt with. The unions are responsible for payment of stewards required for union business.[1] If a shop steward fails to observe the procedure or encourages others to do so, the employer can ask the union to withdraw his credentials.

The agreement sets up a Review Committee to meet at regular intervals (a) to see that all clauses to the agreement are observed; (b) to review productivity; and (c) to review the effect of temporary transfers on the productivity and efficiency of the port. There is also provision for a general review of the agreement in June 1971 to see what improvements in financial and other benefits are justified. Either party can terminate the agreement after a month's notice.

Phase 2 Agreement and the Employers

A later chapter will deal with the views of the unions on the Phase 2 agreement, but two points should be made now about the employers and the agreement. Firstly, the agreement, like the negotiations, reveals the different approaches taken by the PLA and the private stevedores. The first widespread industrial action that followed was a work-to-rule in the Royal and Millwall docks to extend the contingency payments provided for in the Phase 2 agreement; this proved unsuccessful. The PLA opposed these additional payments because their experience of piece-

---

[1] The definition of union business has already proved contentious. Branch, regional, divisional, or national union meetings are considered internal union affairs by management who will not release men on pay. Attendance at meetings of joint bodies of the workers' sides of joint committees are covered only if the management asked for the meeting. Similarly, managers will not pay for shop stewards' meetings at the firm which involve attendance outside normal shift hours, unless they asked for the meeting.

work was that extra payments led to restrictive practices aimed at sharing or monopolizing 'plum' jobs, and that there was pressure to extend them. The PLA wanted freedom to deploy dockers to any job so that they would ultimately possess the full range of skills. By contrast, private stevedores favoured an incentive-based payment system and were primarily concerned with shipwork. Accordingly, they favoured a differential for shipwork, because it is heavier than quay work, whereas the PLA envisaged flexibility between ship and quay. The stevedores also insisted on a specialist allowance for crane drivers for fear that, without it, they would not get volunteers to drive cranes, whereas the PLA felt (rightly as it proved) that payments to some specialist drivers would provoke claims for payments to other machine operators like forklift truck drivers or straddle carriers.

Secondly, the insistence of employers on unilateral discretion over productivity, backed by arbitration, appears to have been totally unrealistic. No arbitration committee was initiated by any employer up to January 1971, because it is almost impossible to prove poor effort in any individual case. At the same time arbitration committees were seen as inappropriate for collective actions like the work-to-rule in October 1970. One PLA manager took the view that, unless they made use of the procedure, the employers would have no argument on productivity grounds for resisting an increase in pay in June 1971. If they complained of low productivity at the review, the unions would say that the dockers could not be to blame or the employers would have used the procedure.

The Formalizing of Industrial Relations
Although the Phase 2 agreement may not suit all employers, the Green Book has a quasi-legal importance as a reference point and arbiter never attained by the Blue Book, its predecessor in Phase 1. Some employers, the PLA in particular, were determined not to let things go as, in retrospect, they felt they had done in Phase 1. This new

c

constitutionalism in collective bargaining has narrowed the scope of custom and practice rules. In the PLA it has also limited the discretion of supervisors and junior managers by moving the level of effective decision-making higher up the hierarchy. One shop steward complained that whereas before he could get effective decisions from his traffic officer or at least from the senior traffic officer in his department, he now had to take issues to the personnel officer or the docks manager, and then they might be referred to the PLA central office. This particular experience may be the consequence of the recent appointment of a new senior traffic officer in that department, but it corresponds very much with what the PLA Industrial Relations Department feels is the authority's resolve to work the agreement and lay down policy explicitly from above. By April 1971 there were some signs of a slight flexibility in the attitude of supervisors over early finishes, possibly sowing the seeds of future custom and practice rules, but the PLA has been aware of such developments elsewhere and checked them.

Although the Green Book marks a new formalism in industrial relations in the London docks and, for the PLA at least, a higher level of effective decision-making, it clearly has not put an end to disputes. Instead it has transferred the argument to the area of interpretation. Managers use the Green Book to justify their decisions but stewards are equally ready to refer to it, and one NASDU steward at Firm A said that there were two interpretations of everything the book contained except money. A shop steward at the PLA said he went home 'dreaming' of the Green Book.

In addition the Green Book does not cover certain areas of dispute such as recruitment and what is and what is not registered dock work.[1] Moreover, the agreement was

---

[1] The 1946 Dock Workers Act gave protections to dockers in work covered by that Act. It did not apply to all ports, however, nor did it determine, as in the case of the packing or unpacking of containers, where

subject to review in June 1971. *All* the parties were aware of this and the dockers, especially at Firm A, seemed to be holding their fire until the review took place. At the PLA both stewards and management accepted that productivity would determine the level of a settlement in that review, but it was not clear whether this was to be productivity for the whole of the port, for the PLA alone, for individual sectors of the PLA, or for individual departments within sectors. For the parties at Firm A the issues were even less clear.

---

dock work ended and other work began. Both these questions were important and not finally settled by 1971, but they fell outside the scope of a study of the effects of the Devlin Committee recommendations on existing registered dock work.

9

Wages

The Phase 2 agreement replaced piecework by time payments and was the first attempt to give the London docks a regulated wage structure. Piecework had generated several pressures and practices and it remained to be seen whether the new wage structure would survive these. Firstly, because piecework was paid on a gang basis with individuals within the gang earning the same piecework payment, unfit or weaker members of the gang were protected. Would they be similarly protected under the new payment system? Secondly, under piecework superior skills should have been reflected in output and hence in earnings, but there was often little relationship between skill and earnings. Would the different skills of dockers all be differentially rewarded under the new wage structure? Thirdly, under piecework opportunities for additional payment were shared by dockers and these imposed restrictions on the allocation of men to jobs. Alternatively, such additional payments were spread to other jobs. Would the additional payments sanctioned by the Green Book lead to similar restrictions and spreading? Finally, piecework bargaining pushed earnings up by as much as thirteen per cent in a single year. What would happen to earnings under the new wage structure?

Protection of the Unfit

The Green Book provides for two categories of worker, A and B, and additional payments to gangers, shipworkers and certain specified machine drivers working as such during a shift. The additional payments for shipwork means that there are three categories of docker; for even where an employer does shipwork and quaywork as the PLA does in South West India Department, shipworkers have traditionally been a separate group.

In fact, the PLA at the South West India Department divides Category A workers into three types (not for differential payment purposes but for greater ease in labour allocation). Grade A_i are full duty dockers fit and ready for shipwork and driving; grade A_{ii} are men fit for general labouring on the quay, but not for driving machines; grade A_{iii} are light duty men. These specifications are also used by shop stewards. It is a reflection of the solidarity among dockers that grade A_i men do not complain about grade A_{iii} receiving the same wage.

Similarly, the gangs at Firm A now allow older and less fit men to be permanent 'pitch men' (the ship's gang men who work on the quay). Such 'pitch' hands are technically part of the ship's gang and are therefore paid £39 a week, although managers believe they should be in category B. In 1971 there were only two category B men out of 240 dockers at Firm A, 29 out of 465 at the PLA South West India Department, and 11 out of 165 at Millwall Department.

The desire to protect weaker members of the piecework gang has been carried over into a system which has abandoned both piecework and, on the quay, gang working as well, but is confined within the firm or department. The payment of pitch hands as shipworkers at Firm A is accepted at that firm but resented by some PLA Millwall quay workers. These are paid £36.50 compared with £39 for shipworkers but, since quay work is highly mechanized at Millwall, an individual quay driver may feed or receive from a whole stevedoring gang. This was one reason for the strike and work-to-rule at the PLA for 'con' payments for fork-lift truck drivers.

Different Skills

Another factor behind the strike (which in the Millwall
and India docks was largely concentrated in the PLA Millwall Department) was the demand that skill in machine
driving should be recognized 'as it is in outside industry',
as a shop steward put it. Some machine driving is so
recognized, e.g. crane driving, but fork-lift driving is not.
A similar type of claim was made by PLA stewards at South
West India Department. The shortage of machine drivers
there occasionally requires that shipworkers should be
assigned to quay work to drive machines. The Green Book
authorizes payment of agreed differentials if any of the
specified work is performed during a given shift. Thus
where shipworkers are pulled off the ship *during* a shift
they receive their ship differential. No objection is raised
against this, or against the payment of the differential to
workers assigned to shipwork late in the shift. But shipworkers are occasionally assigned to the quay for the whole
shift because of the shortage of quay 'pointsmen' (drivers
and other specialists) and they then lose the shipwork
differential. This had led to complaints that men should
not be penalized for their skill. Apparently labour foremen
get round the problem by allocating the men initially to a
ship and then re-allocating them to the quay for the whole
shift, relying on another rule customary under piecework
that a docker should be paid for work allocated and then
withdrawn through no fault of his own. At Firm A a
similar type of claim is made that crane drivers should be
paid a retainer, whether or not actually driving a crane in
a shift, as a recognition of their skill.

The shortage of both shipworkers and machine drivers
in the PLA department at Millwall and South West India
suggests that the differentials are insufficient, but the PLA
aims to overcome the shortage by recruitment, training and
full flexibility and mobility, rather than by further additional payments.

Additional Payments

The Green Book offers two types of additional payment to the basic pay: firstly, differential or 'con' payments for certain jobs; secondly, weekend overtime. Given the background of the piecework system and the work practices of the docks, the Green Book might have been expected to lead to pressures for a fair sharing of jobs offering 'con' payments or overtime, and of any other variable elements in pay; to demands for 'cons' to be extended to jobs similar to those which carried extra payment; and to pressure for the automatic payment of 'cons' to workers skilled in or normally employed on jobs carrying an extra payment.

(1) *Differential Payments*. 'Cons' are sanctioned for work on board ship, as a ganger, and as a crane driver. The PLA and Firm A reveal several examples of 'sharing the sweets', as one manager put it. Because loss of extra payment is involved, the PLA has a rota for withdrawing shipworkers to the quay. Because this is unpopular, Firm A has a rota for breaking up gangs. Neither Firm A nor the PLA allocate ship's units or gangs in strict rotation as they used to under piecework. But one stevedoring firm in the sector does so, on the grounds that it is the most objective way of sharing jobs which still vary in difficulty and the degree of effort involved. At the South West India Department the PLA hopes to rotate the departmental labour force round the department's three areas every three months. Within areas men are moved from shed to shed to ensure a fairly equal spread of types of work. By contrast at the Millwall Department, although the work content differs from shed to shed, the area crews are permanent to their sheds except where managers require them to move.

Shortly after Phase 2 began, there was a request at the PLA for the sharing of the gangers' additional shift payment. However, the PLA hoped to make the gangers into supervisors, and, on the quay, permanent gangers were chosen from volunteers for the post. At the South West India Department gangers on the ship are not permanent,

but each gang or unit has its own regular ganger for occa-
sions when the gang is put on other work.

Crane drivers are traditionally part of a ship's gang.
There is no shortage of work for them either at the PLA
or at Firm A. Since they are permanently employed as
crane drivers, no rota is required, but at Firm A they have
asked for the automatic payment of a 'con' to the firm's
qualified crane drivers even if they are not driving cranes.
At the PLA's South West India Department each ship's
unit has a second crane driver to stand in for the regular
driver. These second drivers have a rota for crane driving
independent of their gangs.

There has been some pressure for the extension of 'cons'
to jobs not covered by the Green Book. At Firm A a foreman shipworker expected that a 'con' might be paid to a
gang's hatchman (the man responsible for co-ordinating
the work of the men in the hold or the crane) and to winch
drivers. But the example of the strongest pressure for the
extension of 'con' payments was the two-day strike, followed
by a work-to-rule, over the issue of 'con' payments to fork-
lift truck drivers in October 1970. The PLA suspects that
this dispute had its origin in the 'stretching', as a traffic
officer put it, of additional payments by stevedoring firms.
It was said that a firm at Tilbury had paid 'cons' to diesel
crane drivers although no payment is prescribed in the
agreement. Another firm was said to have made additional
overtime payments to fork-lift truck drivers prior to, but in
preparation for, Phase 2.

Up to April 1971 this was the only widespread industrial
dispute in London during Phase 2. In the Millwall and
India sector it affected mainly the PLA Millwall Department. This is a highly mechanized quay department
where average earnings have dropped both absolutely and
relatively with Phase 2. Before Phase 2, fork-lift truck
drivers were used to additional payments either as 'cons' or
as overtime orders. Both factors may have played their part
in the dispute which had subsided by the end of October,
although the issue was expected to come up again in the

review of Phase 2. The dockers' demands might have been met either by the payment of a 'con' or by a generous use of overtime.[1] In fact they failed to get either. Supported by two full-time union officials, the docks manager is said to have 'read the riot act' at a general meeting of dockers. Local PLA managers had already been told to be firm on 'cons' and in their use of the discretionary overtime under Schedule 1, and PLA officials feel that this firmness helped them to resist the dockers demands.[2] On the other hand, one steward said that the strike ended on a promise of a more generous use of discretionary overtime, and the relevant minutes of the dock managers' meeting with stewards could be interpreted to carry this meaning.

(2) *Overtime.* Overtime is now restricted to weekend working. When overtime was available daily, gangs would 'box' for overtime—pace the job to ensure getting overtime orders. Although the standard working week was 40 hours, average hours recorded by London dockers prior to Phase 2 were more than 46 hours per week. But these hours were not necessarily all worked, for the practice of 'job and finish' meant that the gang went home as soon as the job was done.

The abolition of daily overtime and the continuity rule has put an end to 'boxing' in London. But employers still keep the overtime orders until towards the end of the week (Friday by preference). This is not so much for fear of 'boxing', but because unforeseen circumstances might prevent

[1] Schedule 1 sanctioned payments for work outside shift work to enable a prompt start to general working. They could be paid to machine drivers for the collection or return of gear outside shift hours.

[2] The PLA figures for quay work allowances, as a percentage of total labour costs, show no trend upwards for the first four months of the scheme:

	Millwall Department	*S.W. India Department*
October 1970	2·8	3·2
November 1970	3·0	3·5
December 1970	2·6	3·5
January 1971	2·0	3·2

work being available at the weekend, and as during Phase 1, overtime has to be paid once the order is given.

In 1969 Firm B's men would not agree to work Saturdays on the same terms as Sundays, and Firm B's managers were therefore surprised at the acceptance of the Green Book provisions on Saturday working. Compared with Sunday, Saturday working is likely to be advantageous to the company by speeding turnaround of the ship, so that dockers might have asked for more. But Saturday shifts were limited to four hours, which probably explains why there has been little Saturday working in the India and Millwall docks, even where there is heavy Sunday working. The PLA managers feel that Saturday working is not economically viable because the shift is so short.

Since overtime is expensive, it is likely to be used only where a quick turnaround is wanted. This explains the unequal distribution of overtime between the Millwall and India parts of the docks. Millwall concentrates on regular shipping lines working a continental trade on a weekly basis. Ships can, if necessary, leave cargo for export to the following week. Thus not much weekend overtime is worked there. By the end of 1970 Firm A had worked no Saturdays and only two Sundays. There is more ocean-going shipping, and in particular for eastern trade, at South West India. Ships' voyages are longer and since they call at several ports, more complicated. Thus Sunday working has been fairly regular at the South West India Department, until the overtime ban by the PLA dockers there in December.[1]

Each firm or department has a formal rota for overtime, but the uneven distribution of overtime has not brought demands for sharing overtime between firms or between the departments of the PLA. The ending of temporary transfers between firms makes a sector rota impossible, but the Millwall PLA dockers might have been

---

[1] In October 450 men at the South West India Department of the PLA worked Sundays, and in November 330. This compares with 2 men in October and 36 men in November in the Millwall Department.

expected to claim some of the Sunday working of the other PLA departments. However, there was not much movement of labour from the Millwall Department even during Phase 1, and it has never been the practice to share overtime among firms or departments.

Within firms and the departments of the PLA the overtime rota is administered strictly on an individual basis. Either a Sunday worked or an offer refused constitutes a turn in the rota and the rota covers the whole labour force, not just dockers working the jobs requiring overtime. Similarly, in the South West India Department the rota for category A men over-rides the preference of some of these men for quay work: if they refuse shipwork on a Sunday, they lose a turn.

This system may run into trouble because of lack of balance in the labour force. Sunday work at South West India has been mainly manual, but if overtime was required primarily on mechanized work like exports, then fork-lift drivers and shipworkers would have to have preference. The works committee at Firm B agreed in 1969 that if overtime was restricted to shipwork then the rota would only operate for their Grade 1 workers to the exclusion of their Grade 2 men who are not available for shipwork. A similar solution seems possible at South West India.

Earnings Under Phase 2
NDLB figures for the final quarter of 1970 show average earnings of slightly over £42 per week for dockers in London. Given a labour force generally employed on basic wages of £36.50 or £39 per week, this constitutes an average earnings level of about ten per cent above basic wages. PLA data for Millwall and India show that their 'con' payments or additional shift allowance constitute between two and three per cent of total labour costs. Consequently, even if stevedores are rather more liberal with 'cons', the major part of the ten per cent gap appears to come from weekly overtime working, which is vulnerable to a drop in trade such as occurred in 1971.

However, overtime has not been spread evenly. In October and November 1970, for example, dockers at the PLA South West India Department earned about £14 a month in weekend overtime. For the same period the average overtime earnings at the Millwall Department were just over £1 a month. In Phase 1, dockers at the Millwall Department were averaging about £40, rather more than at the South West India Department. Under Phase 2 average earnings at Millwall have dropped to about £37.[1] At South West India with its high proportion of shipworkers and greater overtime opportunities, average earnings for October and November 1970 must have been between £41 and £42 per week. These comparisons were clearly an important factor in the Millwall demand for additional payments to all machine drivers. More generally these figures illustrate that increased average earnings under Phase 2 have not brought higher pay to all dockers in London. Nor has the new pay structure put an end to disputes over differentials or to all fluctuations in earnings.

[1] All workers at Millwall are quay workers on a £36.50 basic.

10

Shiftwork

Wages were one aspect of the Phase 2 agreement. Changes in work methods were the other. The next three chapters deal with these under the headings of shiftwork, time-keeping, and the manning of work, and all were affected by the decline in the size of the labour force. This decline was accentuated by the extra week's holiday allowed under the agreement and by the termination of facilities for the temporary borrowing of labour which had allowed the 'flooding' of ships with dockers to ensure a quick turn-around.[1]

The decline of the labour force has had different effects on individual firms. Firm A's labour force has remained fairly constant at about 250 since 1967 while the PLA labour force for the whole of the Millwall and India sector has declined by twenty per cent (1,580 to 1,266), with the South West India Department and Millwall Department losing about thirty and twelve per cent respectively. The most obvious reason for the difference between the PLA and Firm A is the more generous severance scheme of the PLA. The difference between South West India and Mill-wall Departments of the PLA is explained by the fact that Millwall was already a mechanized department in 1967 and had smaller scope for contraction.

It is the PLA, then, which complains of labour shortage. Furthermore, since 1967 ten per cent of the PLA labour

[1] Between the end of 1968 and the summer of 1970 the number of registered dock workers in London had declined by fifteen per cent.

force in the Millwall and India sector has transferred (largely to Tilbury). Any replacements have been men from the London and Surrey docks workers, who, by general consent, are reckoned to lack mechanical skills and are not used to the types of cargo handled at India and Millwall. There is, therefore, a particular shortage of machine drivers. The less serious shortage of shipworkers is expected to increase as more shipworkers opt for the easier jobs on the quay. PLA shop stewards have therefore demanded that new dockers shall either be experienced in machine driving or else go on the ship in the West India Departments, thus releasing shipworkers for machine driving in other departments.

Shiftwork involves new managerial responsibilities. Some dock employers, including the PLA,[1] have reorganized their methods of allocating labour to meet the requirements of shiftwork. All of them now have to decide on the best distribution of dockers in each shift, and to make arrangements for work continuity and co-ordination between shifts. In common with most dock employers, both the PLA and Firm A divide their labour force equally between the morning and afternoon shifts, with the two halves alternating weekly. Individuals can swap shifts with management approval. The PLA Industrial Relations Department says that the equal division was intended to cure dockers of their preference for the morning shift and to put pressure on road hauliers to alter their arrangements to fit in with a shift system. Firm A defended an equal division on the grounds that it would give each shift the same spread of work.

But Firm B, with a longer experience of shift work, has a 2:1 division with each worker doing two weeks of mornings and one week of afternoons in a regular cycle. This suits the dockers and the bulk of the work is done in the morning, leaving the afternoon to complete essential tasks. Another possibility is to arrange overlapping shifts to allow

[1] See Appendix II.

earlier finishes. The departmental management at Millwall confirmed that little work was done towards the end of the afternoon shift since few lorries arrived after 7 p.m. A further defect of an equal division between shifts is that it may have insufficient capacity to give priority treatment to regular customers and urgent orders.

There is no evidence, however, of competition between shifts over work done. Firms do not keep shift output records as a basis for competition. Occasionally workers complain that the previous gang has worked the easiest cargo or the easiest storage parts of the hold, but usually gangs seem to have regard for the next shift, and managers say that the standard of storage has improved.

Shiftwork has brought new problems for dockers as well as for their employers. Like managers, shop stewards do not entertain complaints about the work of the previous shift and advise against competition. However, shop stewards did complain about the lack of adequate co-ordination between shifts. In their view the allocation of labour during the previous shift meant that they could not 'get at' those responsible for errors. But these complaints were only part of a wider criticism of the present manning arrangements and the limited role of shop stewards in their determination.

A more immediate complaint about shiftwork, raised by all the shop stewards, was that it breaks up the labour force thereby hindering unity and communications. Full-time trade union officers suspect that shifts have been used by management to split up militants and a senior traffic officer commented on the reduction in 'mass hysteria' with no more prolonged lunch breaks and shop stewards spending less time together. Shop stewards have difficulty getting their constituents together. Since Phase 2 there have been departmental and sector meetings of PLA workers but these have been short and often poorly attended because pay is lost through attending them, and there is less confidence that decisions will be followed. The shift system has destroyed the newly established works committee at Firm A

which, according to the stewards, was beginning to prove
a useful organ of general work force opinion. The members
are on different shifts and, like PLA dockers, they do not
relish the loss of pay involved in unpaid meetings during
work.[1] Stewards in the same firm or department can
meet only if they come early for the afternoon shift or leave
late on their morning shift. In the South West India
Department they keep a book of issues which arise, for the
stewards on the next shift.[2]

Given the opposition of NASDU and many TGWU
members to the idea of shiftwork, it is to be expected that
stewards would criticise the physical and social effects of
shift work. They complain of changeover difficulties, early
rising for the morning shift, and late return from the afternoon shift, and the generally detrimental effect on family
and social life. Since shiftwork is accepted, these complaints have not led to demands for a return to daywork,
but dockers are sensitive about timekeeping and early
finishes, and their complaints colour their attitude to the
scheme as a whole.

[1] By contrast, when shiftwork was introduced at Firm B in 1969, the
firm put all the workers' representatives on their works committee on the
same shift.

[2] The refusal of the PLA to pay overtime to stewards for coming in
early or leaving late was one factor behind a weekend overtime ban at the
South West India Department at the end of 1970.

Timekeeping

Under piecework, time spent at work was only one element, and a decreasing element, in determining pay. Argument and interest centred on the daily tonnage produced, and the time spent at work was only incidental. Workers took their own decisions on the methods and pace of work. Even overtime became just a unit of payment, governed by the same criteria as other payments, such as comparisons with other gangs and with previous work, the effort put into the job, and precedent.

There was no organized 'welting' or 'spelling'[1] in London, but individuals could be temporarily absent from the job or informal rest periods could be taken. This could happen even with mechanized manning. The PLA Millwall Department used three-men quay gangs for delivery to and from ships. These were composed of a fork-lift truck driver and two board 'boys' (manual assistants to the driver). But only one man was generally required to assist the driver and the board boys therefore took turns 'to have a blow'. Similarly at Firm B, even under the 1967 agreement which replaced gangs with units that were not only smaller than traditional gangs but also expected to be flexibile, the men in the units covered up for absentees. Foremen called this the 'hop' system, for the absentees were 'on the hop'.

How far were the norms developed under the previous system carried over into Phase 2, and with what effect?

[1] These are terms for practices in the ports of Liverpool and Glasgow by which half the gang worked while the other half rested.

Concern for time spent at work, inherent in the Phase 2 agreement, is something new in the docks and might be expected to cause conflict. In explaining his tolerance of early finishing or temporary absence, one foreman said he appreciated that dockers were not clerks, 'they're free men'. Under the new agreement there are three distinct areas of possible controversy: prompt or late starting, unauthorized absence during work, and early finishing.

Starting Work

Penalties for late arrivals are not new, but a shorter working day and the increased responsibility of management for getting the job done might be expected to lead to greater strictness. Practice varies in fact. Methods of allocating labour and the point at which men muster both affect the recording of lateness and absence. If men muster at a central point, time must be allowed for the supervisor to book the men in and for the men to move off to the sheds or ships where they are working. Less time should be needed if they muster with the foreman at the shed or ship, and both Firm A and the PLA instruct men to muster with the foreman. This causes no difficulty in those parts of the PLA where men are permanent to an area or a shed. Otherwise orders have to be given overnight so that the men know where to go, and this is done whenever possible at Firm A. Further complications arise in large firms because certain categories of workers muster centrally for collection of mechanized gear. Arrangements are therefore governed by the variability and predictability of work and the size and geographical spread of the firm. But the experience of Firm B shows that the time saved by mustering with operational foremen can be exaggerated. Foremen found they had to allow men time, after they had mustered, to get their overalls or otherwise prepare for work.

Supervisors are not uniformly strict in recording arrival at work. A shed foreman or foreman shipworker is more likely to miss specialist machine drivers and record their late arrival than unspecialized manual workers and the attitudes of supervisors vary. PLA stewards complain of differences between labour co-ordinators and foremen shipworkers on the one hand, and shed foremen on the other. Stewards feel that the labour co-ordinators and foremen shipworkers, having worked as dockers, understand them and know the men personally so that they can allow discretion in 'genuine' cases. Shed foremen are drawn from clerical staff and lack experience and personal knowledge. In addition, the stewards claim that the end of piecework has increased the responsibilities of the shed foremen, and this 'new power has gone to their heads'. There are complaints that shed foremen treat men like numbers and are unreasonably strict about a few minutes' absence. Accordingly, the stewards wanted more labour co-ordinators at the South West India Department so that there could be central mustering under their control. However, the stewards tended to overstate their case. It is not true that all shed foremen lack operational experience and understanding of dockers. It was a shed foreman who pointed out that dockers are 'free men'. Moreover, all foremen are subject to conflicting pressures. A foreman at Firm B who had been a docker said that when he was responsible for the muster he felt inclined to overlook the occasional late arrival of a 'genuine' man (one not usually late), but if he did so the habitual late arriver would complain of unfair treatment if he was 'booked'. He expressed relief that mustering at Firm B now takes place centrally under one administrative foreman.

In any case, the ban on 'early mornings' for gear collection at the PLA, and the failure of ancillary services such as lighterage and road haulage to suit their times to shiftwork, has led to delays and has reduced the importance of prompt arrival at work.

Unauthorized Absence

The incidence of unauthorized absence depends on the size of the working unit. The 'hop system' at Firm B has been reduced by the break-up of the units which makes covering up more difficult. Similarly, the abolition of three-handed gangs on the quay at the PLA Millwall Department and the new norm of $1\frac{1}{2}$ men per fork-lift truck has put an end to the 'blow' for board men. At Firm A, by contrast, traditional manning remains largely undisturbed. The men there send out scouts to discover the state of work in the firm at the various parts of the dock. The foremen shipworkers either turn a blind eye or are not aware that the scouts are absent. It is a measure of the failure of the firm to make gangers part of the management that the gangers will not 'sneak' on absentees. Managers at Firm A expressed disappointment that the works committee would not take responsibility for disciplining absentees although they believe many of the men would like to see the firm do something about these who 'take liberties'.

Finishing Times

As with other aspects of timekeeping, practice concerning finishing times varies within firms and between firms, but by the end of 1970 most firms were allowing a degree of 'discretion', especially on the afternoon shift. In various firms and in different parts of the same firm, 7.30 p.m., 8 p.m., or 8.15 p.m. were seen as 'reasonable' last times for changing jobs. While there are no precise records of average finishing times, it was generally believed that men working for stevedores finished work earlier than men working for the PLA.

These differences in finishing times are affected by the size of the firm and the variety of its operations. 'Job and finish' was said to be less prevalent in larger stevedoring firms than in smaller firms, and the PLA feels itself better placed than the stevedores to use the full shift because its larger and more varied operations provide alternative work to offer the men. There is usually a job available such as re-stowing or re-housing cargoes in sheds for future deliveries. However, even the PLA is limited when work is slack or when ancillary services are not available. The Millwall Department complained that slackness was caused by no lorries arriving after 7 p.m.

Large firms also have more elaborate controls. One large stevedoring firm had a system whereby men had to hand in cards at a central labour office when they left, whereas a small firm working from the same shed with closer personal contact between man and management, took decisions on early departures 'on the site.' But policy is important too. The PLA is said to create work to keep men in, but by the end of 1970 PLA supervisors were being allowed some discretion, with decisions being taken by the traffic officer in some instances and in others by the shed foreman and the foreman shipworker. At Firm A, in contrast, foremen shipworkers cannot allow men to go home, but must send them to the superintendent.

Managers at Firm A feel that 7.30 p.m. is a reasonable last time for change of jobs. They allow half an hour for job change, 20 minutes to uncover a new hatch, and 20 minutes to recover before the end of the shift. Consequently, if these allowances are accurate, a 7.30 p.m. job change leaves only 20 minutes working time. The managers fear that if they tried to change jobs later than 7.30 p.m. the men would pace the previous job to finish at 8 p.m. or 8.15 p.m. and then a delay due to weather or technical breakdowns could mean the job would not be finished by 9 p.m. Foreman shipworkers at the PLA said that it was unreasonable to start a new job later than 1 p.m. on the morning shift and 8 p.m. in the evening, and shed foremen said 8.15 p.m. was the last time a ship's gang would be moved to quay work.

These examples require a job to be a definable piece of work. In conventional dock work men perform one operation, such as the clearing of a hold or the loading of a lorry, but where work is mechanized there is no 'discrete' job. Foremen at Millwall said that with mechanization, units could be delivering to the quay, returning with imports, and storing in sheds in successive operations. Thus if delivering imports or exports ceased, they would still have work to do. Elsewhere a non-mechanized gang would, for example, be receiving from a ship's hold only, so that when this finished they would have to be moved to find them new work.

The practice of 'job and finish' can be used as a kind of incentive payment. While admitting restrictions on re-allocating men after certain times in the shift, foremen ship-workers at Firm A and the PLA said they were adamant in their refusal to offer men either job and finish or a given tonnage and finish. If they offered job and finish, jobs might be rushed and finished by 6 p.m. or even earlier. New standards of early finish might then be established leading to claims for early finishing even when the job was not finished, on the grounds that it was exceptionally awkward or difficult. Next there would be claims for a rota to share jobs which finish particularly early and objections to the breaking down of gangs where such finishes are involved. On the other hand, if tonnage norms were established, then men would argue 'we would have done x tons but . . .' as they did under piecework. Either way formal job and finish practices would bring back some of the worst aspects of the piecework system for management.

Nevertheless, practices vary not only between firms and departments but even between sheds and areas within departments. Why are these differences tolerated? One reason is that practices do not vary greatly. Another is lack of knowledge: there is little movement of labour even within departments and certainly between departments so that marginal differences in finishing times are not noticed. Although stewards at the South West India Department have queried why some foremen are less flexible than others, stewards do not generally initiate complaints, and shed foremen say they would ignore comparisons with other sheds. Perhaps the dockers in each area or shed are willing to live with different finishing times as they formerly accepted different informal agreements on piecework allowances and different variations of the continuity rule.

However, the PLA stewards take note that their finishing times are generally later than those of the stevedores' men, as one of several adverse comparisons. They do not ask for comparable finishing times, for this would be illegitimate under the Green Book, but they use the difference in arguments against managers when these complain about the output of PLA men. The comparison was also used to support the claim that the PLA should negotiate a separate agreement in June 1971. In addition, the stewards say they note any arrangements for overmanning and nonproductive work made in order to keep men at work until the end of the shift, as grounds for questioning management's productivity figures.

Analytically distinct from early finishing, at least in managers' eyes, is the situation when lack of work allows men to have all or part of the shift off with pay. Firm B works a rota for days off, giving notice beforehand, but once a shift has started early finishes are left to the luck of the draw. Firm A also works a rota for days off, but does not give prior notice. Although there is no rota for exceptionally early finishes, a note is taken for use in future allocation of work. The PLA has not yet faced this situation because it has been able to keep its men more fully employed.

The failure of some firms to provide work for their men to last the whole of a shift weakens their complaints about dockers' poor timekeeping. In January 1971 the LOTEA produced figures[1] on time lost during a shift which threw additional doubt on the culpabilitity of the dockers. Most of the time lost can be ascribed to management's failure to ensure a steady flow of work and machines. In addition, transport delays account for twice as much time lost as the one factor entirely within the control of the dockers—extended meal breaks.

[1] Late starts due to making ready, opening sheds, providing equipment—30 min.; extension of meal breaks—15 min.; early finishes—20 min.; transport delays—30 min.; weather—30 min.; equipment delays—20 min. Total time lost per seven hour shift—2 hr. 5 min. (*Guardian*, 14 January 1971).

One PLA manager claimed that he had been amazed at the timekeeping of the men at the beginning of Phase 2. In spite of lack of public transport, the first shift turned up to work on time at 7 a.m. and the second shift worked through to 9 p.m. However, when they began to find that work was not ready to start at 7 a.m.; when they saw work practically stopped from noon to 1.30 p.m. to suit the hours of work of lightermen and lorry drivers; and when they saw work practically finished at 7 p.m.; the dockers' attitude to timekeeping became more casual.

12

The Manning of Work

Together with shift work, flexibility and mobility of labour were the *quid pro quo* for the high basic rates offered in the Green Book. Prior to Phase 2 dockers imposed restrictions on the minimum size of a gang for a given task, on the number of gangs on any operation, on the movement of gangs from one task to another, and on the separation of individuals from their gangs. The employers did not undertake any costing of these practices such as occurred, for example, in the USA prior to the 1960 West Coast agreement, but they believed that the costs were high. Some employers, however, particularly the stevedores, seemed to apply little pressure to get rid of these practices. It was technological change which rendered them totally inappropriate to employers using mechanized equipment. In any case improvement in ship design and mechanical aids were undermining traditional manning levels, but the impetus for sweeping them away came from radical improvements in techniques of handling. Even before Phase 1, terminal agreements at Firm B in the Millwall dock and in several berths at Tilbury had involved radical changes in labour practices. In addition there had been reductions in manning at several quay departments like the Millwall Department of the PLA. The mechanization of cargo handling, such as pre-packaged bulk cargoes and side loading with its high capital cost, was the cause of all these changes, and the negotiations over Phase 2 were hastened by the 'container ban'.[1]

[1] See Chapter 7.

Gang Working and Gang Sizes

Technology had thus determined the extent of change
under Phase 2. Mechanized handling permits individual
working, whereas traditional handling required working
in teams or gangs. Quay work is generally more amenable
to mechanization than shipwork and the PLA says it has
achieved individual working on the quay since Phase 2.
Mechanization had already affected quay work before
Phase 2. At the Millwall Department gangs of 3 or 6 had
replaced gangs of 10 and 14 for shed-to-quay and trans-
port-to-shed operations, but these reduced gangs have now
given way to individual operation. In more traditional
departments such as the South West India Department, the
change has been more dramatic, and in two specific areas
there have been reductions in manning from 55 to 18 and
from 21 to 8 men. The difference between ship and quay
work in their suitability for mechanization helps to explain
the contrasting records of the PLA and the private stevedores on manning, but there are differences between them
even where they undertake similar operations.

One traffic officer in the South West India Department
said that units of as small as 5 men are being put out to
ship on pre-palletized work, and he now works on a basic
unit of 8 for ships, compared with 10 previously. Additional workers are added for some types of work, such as
the delivery of canned goods overside to barges (12 men)
and some ships' lockers (10 for delivery to quay and 12
overside). Another PLA foreman shipworker maintained
the traditional units of 10 and 12 men for conventional
ships, because, in his opinion, output would otherwise fall.
But he said that there are now no set gangs. Smaller units
would be put on if the job required fewer men or else if
fewer men were available.

Firm A works on a division of their labour force into 18
gangs of 10 compared with 12 gangs of 12 before. Gangs
are never allowed to fall below 10, and, according to one
shipworker, gang sizes are in fact the same as before
Phase 2. Previously, surplus workers were added to units

of 12. Now more surplus workers are added to units of 10. The final size of gang is, therefore, much the same as before.

Flexibility and Mobility

PLA traffic officers and foremen shipworkers find their new authority to break down gangs during work quite as important as their discretion to vary gang sizes. The size of ships' gangs is altered as the work content of the hold changes. At the PLA there are no restrictions on splitting gangs or on taking individuals off the ship and putting them on the quay. It is said that men complain if they are moved from hatches while work is still being done there, and managers say that it makes sense to keep a man at a particular hatch for a full shift or even for several shifts if the job lasts that long, because of his acquaintance with the job. But they are adamant that no restrictive practices are developing.

When handling general and mixed cargo, Firm A puts on enough men to cover the worst of the job. Since men do not like being moved, they stretch the number in the gangs to reduce the necessity for movement between gangs. Occasionally they break down a gang on the job, but this is rare enough to allow them to operate an individual rota for men leaving their gangs.

These variations in planned and actual gang sizes and in policies on breaking gangs down cannot be ascribed to technological variations alone. There are at least three other reasons for differences in managerial practice. These are the labour supply situation of the firm in relation to its trade, its costing system, and the ability and attitude of its supervisors.

The PLA has found itself short of labour to cover all its operations in the South West India and Millwall Departments and is particularly short of shipworkers and machine drivers, whereas Firm A has had the problem of keeping its labour force occupied. Consequently, the PLA has been inclined to pare gang sizes down to the minimum, to reduce the number of working points, and to break down existing working units when men are required more urgently elsewhere. Firm A have been inclined to 'fill up' their gangs to cover all eventualities and to avoid the need to break down existing units.

The PLA charges its customers on tonnage rates so that a reduction in man hours per ton increases its profit margin. The private stevedores are working a temporary 'cost-plus' system until they can establish new tonnage rates. They charge direct labour costs (man hours of dockers employed on the given job) plus ninety per cent to cover NDLB charges, indirect labour costs, and profit margin. Since they must pay their workers a weekly wage even if there is no work for them, it is clearly to their advantage to fill up ships with men. This costing system is in direct conflict with the aims of the Phase 2 on manning and flexibility, and, if the stevedores' new tonnage rates are based on present costs, they will be unrealistic.

Labour supply and costing systems influence management policies on manning, but these policies are also influenced by management beliefs about the 'right way' to operate. With manning as with 'con' payments, the PLA differ from the stevedores in their determination 'to work to the book'. For example the PLA Millwall Department rejected a request from the stewards for a manning norm of two men per fork-lift truck on the grounds that the Green Book forbade any fixed manning.

This contrast between the PLA and the stevedores is matched by differences between their stewards. The stevedores maintain that they are still subject to restrictions. The stewards at Firm A say that before Phase 1 began they were promised conventional manning on conventional jobs. If a manager does not honour this arrangement, 'experience keeps him in order', said one steward.

At the PLA, however, neither managers nor the Industrial Relations Department complained of restrictive manning policies. On the contrary, they expressed surprise at the flexibility they had achieved. Although the stewards at the Millwall Department complained that management had not kept their promise of at least 90 men per shift they have taken no retaliatory action. Stewards at the PLA raise objections to particular decisions on manning and to particular job orders, but only, they say, to decisions which result in a drop in productivity, such as putting out gangs too small for the job or putting out gangs to provide work for surplus labour. These complaints are made because the stewards would like to have a say in manning and labour allocation.

Several reasons can be suggested for these differences between the two groups of stewards. The stevedoring stewards were contemptuous of the operational experience and ability of their managers, regarding the senior supervisors as newcomers and outsiders to the industry, 'riding on the backs' of shipworkers and dockers; whereas although they had doubts about shed foremen, the PLA stewards did not question the ability of their other supervisors. PLA stewards felt that the restrictions applied in stevedoring firms were intended by the men to 'retain something to sell' in the June 1971 review: whereas they themselves felt they could justify a pay increase then on broader productivity grounds. In addition, stevedoring stewards feared that general reductions in manning would lead to unemployment. The differences could also reflect conflicts of union policy in the Phase 2 negotiations since the TGWU cover an overwhelming majority of PLA employees and NASDU are concentrated almost exclusively among the private stevedoring firms.

However, these differences do not seem to be as important as the contrast in managerial policies. Given that the PLA have attempted to reduce manning and increase flexibility, the stewards have felt bound under the Green Book to accept the policy while arguing for collective control of labour allocation and productivity measurement. Firm A has had no general policy of reducing manning. This has confirmed their dockers' belief in the firm's incompetence and justified the stewards in rejecting occasional attempts at reductions as unfair to the individuals concerned and contrary to the norm which the management has established.

Job Demarcation

Besides the mobility of individuals between working units, managers want flexibility to tackle operations in the order which suits them. Where mechanization has led to individual working, this flexibility has generally been achieved. At the Millwall Department even the managers are surprised at the way dockers have been taking out exports and bringing back imports in successive operations. Given this connection between individual working and flexibility, it might be supposed that the continued use of stable teams on conventional operations would help to maintain restrictions on flexibility such as the continuity rule. In fact, all three firms deliberately send out men who are used to working together, not because the men prefer it but because the firms feel that their performance is improved by their confidence in each other. Nevertheless the restrictions have largely gone. Their rationale lay in the pursuit of stability and equality in working conditions under piecework.

Dockers are still interested in equality under Phase 2. Formal or informal rotas for the distribution of additional payments (overtime and 'cons') and of especially onerous work like bag work still place a check on flexibility. However, these restrictions seem trivial compared with the division of work between shipwork and quay work imposed on the industry in general in London, which ensures that work continues to be double-handled. Certainly where employers have consistently tried to change work practices, dockers have not been unco-operative.

13

Supervision

Termination of a piecework system often creates a need for more and better supervision. This need might be expected to be at its strongest in the London docks. Not only was the pace of work determined by the dockers but their control was reinforced by their manipulation of manning scales and work practices.

In retrospect, Phase 1 was a special period for supervision. Under the casual system gangers and foremen had considerable authority because of their power to 'hire and fire'. Gangers were working dockers chosen with their gangs by foremen. The authority of the gangers rested on their ability to select the members of their gangs.[1] The foremen quay gangers and foremen shipworkers derived their authority from choosing gangs for particular jobs. Both sources of authority declined with Phase 1 and decasualization (though the decline had probably begun before that in the PLA). Gangers no longer selected their men, and foremen no longer hired gangs. The smallness of the additional payments (or 'con') for gangers under Phase 1 weakened their position further and led to the resignation of a number of permanent gangers from the PLA. Foremen were often by-passed in piecework negotiation and their loss of disciplinary powers was emphasized by the failure of senior management to support their disciplinary decisions.

[1] One stevedore suggested that a 'good' ganger would 'get through a gang in two years', i.e. exhaust them by work in chasing the highest paying jobs.

What happened to supervision under Phase 2? At
Firm A there seemed to have been little change since
Phase 1. There has been no pressure from supervisors to
change manning scales or to exercise greater control over
the operation of work; the dockers would have stopped
them if they had tried. Workers are still allocated to jobs
by the superintendents who are not drawn from the ranks
of foremen shipworkers. This is resented both by the foremen shipworkers and by the men as an obstacle to promo-
tion. Foremen shipworkers complain that little attention is
paid to their comments on the workers allocated to them.
The superintendents think that only half the shipworkers
are up to their jobs, but hope ultimately to involve them
in labour allocation. They have no intention of involving
the gangers whom they see as part of the labour force. The
firm claims to have appointed permanent gangers but these
gangers continue to work with their regular gangs and
there has been no change in their position.

In the PLA the position of some foremen and gangers
has changed radically. The position of gangers at the PLA
now varies between ship and quay. On the quay a fixed
number of permanent gangers cover the working areas.
They are not yet paid as staff but the intention is that
they should be. There are fewer gangers than before
because of the abolition of gangs and the reduction of
manning. In both the Millwall and South West India
Departments there is one quay ganger to each shed foreman, and the foremen and traffic officers think that this
is enough. PLA senior managers admitted that quay
gangers are not yet part of the management team although
they attend labour allocation meetings at the smallest area
of the South West India Department. The senior traffic
officer there would like to see this arrangement in other
areas. So far the size and variety of their operations have
prevented it, but the gangers are consulted by the traffic
officers. Gangers are not involved in labour allocation at
the Millwall Department and there is no prospect of this

happening. Being a highly mechanized department with
a steady work flow, Millwall has less need for formal allocation meetings. PLA ships' gangers are not permanent.
Managers see them as part of the labour force which is
allocated, not as having any part in allocating it.

Many PLA foremen have good relations with their
gangers but one foreman at the Millwall Department said
he was not happy about the gangers allocated to him and
so gave them little scope for supervision. A shipworker at
the South West India Department said that replacements,
largely from the Surrey and London docks, were not
acquainted with their new work.

Shed foremen at the PLA are now promoted from assis-
tant foremen on ability and not, as before, by seniority.
Under Phase 1 the shed foremen was often desk-bound
and the foreman quay ganger (now labour co-ordinator)
was responsible for operational control. The labour co-
ordinator is mainly concerned with drawing up the lists of
workers from supervisors' requirements, whereas the shed
foremen now spend six of the seven hours a shift on the
job. They find their work less frustrating because they
now say what jobs are to be done. They deploy labour and
sort out 'bottlenecks'.

Foremen shipworkers at the PLA were always involved
in operational control. The only change under Phase 2
in this respect is that closer supervision is required to maintain workers' effort. However, foremen shipworkers, like
shed foremen, are now responsible for recording tons per
man-hour each shift, and they do not all take readily to this
task. Along with their work on rotas for crane drivers and
withdrawing individuals from the ship, this obligation
means that they have, if anything, less direct contact with
the work than before. Perhaps this explains why one traffic
officer said that although he could safely leave shed work
to the shed foreman, he needed to supervise shipwork more
closely.

Dockers have not always reacted favourably to these

D

changes in the role of supervisors. PLA shop stewards
resented the new powers of the shed foremen. They also
objected to the opening of the new post of labour co-
ordinator to staff as well as to dockers. They asked for an
increase in the number of gangers and of labour co-
ordinators, and for the labour co-ordinators to be given sole
responsibility for booking on. They wanted the labour co-
ordinators' time to overlap both shifts so that someone with
responsibility for any mistakes made on one shift should be
able to see the effects on the next.

Dockers at both the PLA and Firm A are supposed to
take direct orders only from shipworkers and gangers, who
were once dockers and have been 'educated by the men'.
At Firm A practice follows theory and no direct orders are
given by superintendents, but a PLA shed foreman at
South West India said that his orders were accepted by his
men; and a foreman at the Millwall Department said that
while he usually gave orders through his gangers, if the
gangers demurred, he gave the orders direct to the men.

This development is one reason why PLA stewards
wanted more gangers on the quay and a greater involvement of gangers in labour allocation and manning. The
gangers themselves would also like to be involved, and
to have more information on the priorities, finance, and
future of the department and company.

The senior traffic officer at South West India apparently
agreed with his shop stewards on the need for more gangers
and the involvement of gangers in allocation. But he
wanted to include gangers in the management team,
and to pay them staff salaries, whereas stewards wanted
the gangers to be involved as the first step towards greater
participation by workers in decisions previously reserved for
managers.

Generally, the position of supervisors in Phase 2, is
related to the policy of their firms. Where a firm has a
policy to change manning and work practices, the work
expected of a supervisor, at least by his superiors and other

supervisors, has changed. In general supervisors have welcomed such changes as giving them an authority they previously lacked. But even where supervisors do have a new role and authority, the traditional ambivalence in the position of the ganger, as representative of the work force and as first-line supervisor, has not been resolved.

14

Shop Stewards

The relationship between shop stewards and their union is the subject of a later chapter. This chapter deals with their part in the operation of the Phase 2 agreement and the development of labour policy.

Elected workers' representatives on the job were recognized by the PLA even before Phase 1, but not by most of the stevedores. Now recognition is universal. The Green Book sets out the minimum number of duty (full-time) stewards according to the size of the firm, but firms may have more at their discretion. The PLA allows each department one duty steward on quay and one on ship for each shift. Thus there are four shop stewards at the South West India Department representing about 420 men and 2 at Millwall (where the PLA does no ship work) representing about 160 men. Previously at South West India there were 2 full-time and 2 working representatives, and one full-time and one working representative at Millwall. All but one of the present stewards was previously a representative. Firm A was asked for four duty stewards and allowed three for a labour force of about 250.[1] All stewards were to be duty stewards for the first two months and the period could be extended. By January 1971 all of them were still duty stewards.

Previously a full-time representative was paid the average piece-work earnings of his own gang, or of a selected gang or manning point. Now stewards are paid the Green Book

[1] It subsequently reduced this number to two duty stewards in February 1971.

90

rates of those they represent. For stevedores' stewards this is £39 a week. At a mixed PLA department like South West India half of the stewards are supposed to cover ship-work and so receive £39, while the other half receive £36.50 as stewards of quay workers. But since the two jobs overlap, the 'quay' stewards object to this differential.

Two of the stewards at the South West India Department have been workers' representatives for 18 years, one for 10 years and one for 3 years; one steward at the Mill-wall Department has been a representative for 18 years and the other for only 6 months. However, the last-mentioned steward replaced another of 10 years standing who moved to Tilbury and he himself had previously been shop steward for the granary (now demolished) at the Millwall Department. None of the long-servers are subject to periodic re-election, though the Green Book provides for it. They say they can be removed by a mass meeting and take their long service as a sign of confidence. The new steward, who is the only NASDU member among the PLA stewards, was elected by a small majority in a three-cornered contest in which only thirty-five per cent voted.

Prior to decasualization the PLA stewards were 'perms' and at the South West India Department they were permanent gangers. One steward said that the following they had as good gangers helped them to become representatives. During Phase 1 they were heavily involved in piece-work negotiations. However, all the old gangers resigned during Phase 1 in protest at their small 'con' payment. Not all the new gangers were capable of handling negotiations so former gangers often took them over.

All three stewards at Firm A were elected in February 1970. Under NASDU rules stewards are subject to re-election annually, but they expected that their period of office would be extended for another year to cover the negotiations on the review of Phase 2. Their predecessors under Phase 1 had spent most of their time in piecework negotiations. Two of them were not reinstated, and the third declined to stand again, although he has since become a member of the NASDU executive committee.

The stewards' job has changed now that piecework has gone. Some managers suggested that stewards have nothing to do and therefore look for trouble. One senior manager added that because of this he preferred to use gangers as a means of communication with the dockers. One steward admitted to being bored and anxious to leave, but stewards denied that they had to look for trouble. They claimed trouble was always brewing. The PLA stewards said they worked 'full out' to prevent a 'blow up' on the introduction of Phase 2 and their union officer said that stewards in general had done an essential job, largely in their own time, to make sure that the agreement worked.

PLA stewards still take up individual grievances with managers on lateness, absence from work, rotas and working conditions. They have monthly meetings with the docks manager and see him in between as issues arise. They meet together on their own before seeing him. They may object to a particular manning arrangement, and they have authority to check productivity records. This enables them to complain about the misrecording of work and to criticise specific manning methods. But they would like a still greater say in the allocation of labour, shift by shift.

Firm A stewards also handle individual issues, but refuse to consider joint disciplinary arrangements. They would like to see safety committees but they do not press for a greater say in manning or labour allocation because it seems to them that the firm's management has no autonomy in this area.

Whether stewards look for disputes or not, they themselves have been the cause of disputes in Phase 2. Final agreement has not been reached on the number of duty stewards; the question of weekend overtime for duty stewards led to an overtime ban at the end of 1970; and the stewards' grievance about unpaid overtime was still unsettled.

Shop Stewards and Labour Policy

During Phase 1 the behaviour of the stewards was governed by the daily piecework negotiations. The disputes associated with that system would have arisen even if there had been no stewards, and there is little evidence that the stewards went further afield than before in seeking comparisons to quote in piecework disputes.

The PLA stewards have a sector joint shop steward committee which meets before the stewards' meetings with the docks manager. Its minutes do not suggest that the stewards were seeking to generalize concessions or to look for new precedents. The PLA stewards make no attempt to combine with the stevedores' stewards, although if arbitration committtees ever get going, they may lead to meetings between the two groups. Stevedores' stewards maintain regular informal contact among themselves.

The PLA stewards have representatives on the PLA Group Joint Committee, the TGWU No. 1 Docks Group, and the Enclosed Docks Group Joint Committee, and they report back to the stewards' meetings. Firm A's stewards have no representatives on the Ocean Trades Group Committee though one of Firm A's employees (the ex-steward) is on the executive of NASDU. The Port Liason Committee[1] is dead, and even when active it had little influence with the PLA stewards at the Millwall and South West India sector.

Despite these fairly haphazard arrangements, a steward at Firm A said that the docks had the 'best grapevine of any industry in the country' and it seemed to be possible to discover the working practices of any firm or sector in London over the telephone. Internal communications within the firm or department were less satisfactory. All the stewards complained that shiftwork hindered contact with

[1] The Port Liaison Committee was an unofficial body centred on the Royals sector of the London docks. It was accused of being politically motivated, being led by Jack Dash, a self-proclaimed Communist. Whether this was so or not, it acted as an organizer of unofficial industrial action, particularly in the Royals but elsewhere as well.

their constituents and the holding of meetings. When the
PLA stewards hold meetings now, they are briefer and less
well attended than before, and consequently carry less
weight.

There is some divergence of policy among stewards,
both among firms and within firms. PLA stewards are
aware that stevedores have developed different practices
under Phase 2, but (except for the forklift truck issue) they
have not tried to introduce these practices into their own
firms. Instead they used them to support their claim for
separate negotiations in the June 1971 review. In November
1970 the NASDU started a series of one-day strikes for
branch meetings in working time, and then stopped them.
The TGWU stewards agreed with the claim but were not
prepared to strike either officially or unofficially. In January
1971 both unions were pressing the issue at the Enclosed
Docks Group Joint Committee. The work-to-rule over fork-
lift drivers revealed divergences even between departments
in the PLA. As with the continuity issue in 1967, the men
at the Royals sector pursued industrial action (in this case
a work-to-rule) much longer than at the Millwall and India
sector, and within this sector the work-to-rule was concentrated on the Millwall Department.

The stewards see parochialism as an essential feature of
the docks. Issues and tactics vary from sector to sector, firm
to firm, and department to department, and one steward
suggested that decasualization had heightened these
sectional divisions by sharply diminishing movement of
labour between sectors. But sectors or firms are not completely isolated in their industrial action. PLA stewards said
they would use gains in other sectors against their own
management and would support other groups if their backs
are to the wall. Some of them saw the Royals as a battle-
ground for the whole of London because the stevedoring
employers were concentrated there.

15

Productivity

This section concludes with a chapter on productivity under Phase 2. The subject is important for two reasons: firstly, productivity is a criterion by which employers and others judge the success or failure of the scheme; secondly, productivity was to be the basis of the review of port wages under the scheme in June 1971. Only a few of the important questions about the measurement of productivity seem to have been asked so far, let alone answered. Some of these questions suggest themselves from the description of the operation of Phase 2.

Firstly, how is productivity to be measured? The throughput of tonnage is only a measure of *production* in the docks. But even so what tonnage is relevant? Should it be deadweight tonnage only, or measurement tonnage (as under piecework) to allow for variation in the densities of different types of cargo? Is final throughput to be recorded, or the tons moved in any operation of dockwork? The latter would mean, for example, measuring tonnage twice for cargo replaced into a ship's hold or rehoused in a shed after being moved. Next, to convert production figures to a measure of labour productivity it would be necessary to divide the tonnage by the total man-hours involved in moving the cargo. But which men and which of the hours they work are to be considered productive for this purpose? Are workers not directly connected with the movement of tonnage, e.g. shedmen and gearmen, to be included on this side of the calculation or are non-productive workers to be excluded? Are all the shift hours of the relevant men to be included or are their non-productive hours to be excluded? If the latter, which hours are to be considered non-productive? Time lost through bad weather, machine breakdown, waiting for lorries or lighterage craft might be excluded by mutual agreement (though the length of time lost in each category might prove contentious). More contentious still might be the time 'lost' through the double-handling of cargo or necessary preparatory work.

Given these likely areas of argument in the measurement of productivity, it becomes important to know *who* is to measure productivity. Is it to be management alone or is it to be done jointly? If done jointly, what is to be the level of worker participation? Is it to be trade union officials, shop stewards or workers themselves? This question leads to another : is productivity to be measured for the port as a whole? Or is each sector or each company, or each department within the PLA to use its own records for individual claims?

These problem areas are not (as of April 1971) very far advanced towards a solution. The Green Book laid down port productivity as the standard for the port review of the scheme in June 1971. The successor of the Enclosed Docks Modernization Committee, namely the Enclosed Docks Joint Industrial Committee, has a review sub-committee for this purpose, but it had not sat by April 1971. It is to be guided by a joint working party set up in February 1971 and charged with responsibility for setting up the guidelines of performance and productivity and advising the parties on what common information should be fed to it. The working party is also to receive returns of figures from the parties, to monitor them and to encourage companies to investigate the reasons for poor productivity where these were not explained. It is in these latter functions that the working party was to supervise the establishment of joint productivity committees at each company and each sector. Such committees could provide a new institutional framework for collective bargaining in the docks.

Up until April 1971, after many meetings, the working party had only agreed on the heads of information required and asked for its first batch of information from the individual firms; it had not analyzed the information. There was no agreement on what sort of information was required for comparison with earlier periods or indeed whether it would be practical to seek such information; a member of the working party doubted whether it would be available. Sector or company joint productivity committees had not yet been set up. Until they are established and review the figures going up to the working party, it is doubtful whether the labour representatives of the working party will accept them.

That no arrangements for measuring productivity were made before Phase 2 began would be surprising—particularly since the record of Phase 2 was to be compared with the previous period—if it were it not so typical of the general run of employers in the London docks. Their unpreparedness stands in sharp contrast to the measures taken by port employers on the West Coast of America prior to their 1960 agreement. As the measurement of productivity is obviously necessary for the planning and achievement of productivity improvements, this lack of preparedness reflects the employers' failure to decide what they expect or, indeed, want to achieve as a result of the Phase 2 agreement. This parallels the lack of new initiatives in labour policy by some employers after Phase 2.

Despite this general level of unpreparedness, some employers—notably the PLA—have been keeping records on a shed by shed basis so that they could identify sources and causes of poor productivity and bottlenecks in the flow of work. These have enabled working arrangements in different PLA departments to be compared.

In the absence of port *productivity* figures, a great deal of publicity has been given to figures of the weekly tonnages of general cargo handled by each sector of the London enclosed docks and for the enclosed docks of the port as a whole, as evidence of the failure of the Devlin Committee's recommendations in London. Graphs of movements in these tonnages for the first six months of Phase 2 are reproduced below. The pre-Phase 2 standard is the comparable average weekly tonnage for the six months prior to Phase 2.

The figures published exclude the tonnages of container traffic and of PLA tenants who lease berths. They thus exclude the most mechanized cargoes. The drop in trade recorded is a drop only in less mechanized cargoes and this may well have been compensated by an increase in mechanized cargo. No figures were available for the size of the increase in mechanized cargo but *The Port* reported record tonnages in Tilbury's container and bulk transport berths with the end of the container ban.[1] Thus the figures produced might show not a *drop* in the *total* trade of London but a *shift* from non-mechanized to mechanized trade. This shift would be all the more sudden because of the previous two-year ban on new methods of cargo handling imposed by the TGWU until Phase 2 was negotiated.

It must be stressed that the graphs show tonnage figures for the port and these are not the same as productivity figures. Where the firms studied have kept records these show that labour productivity has been remarkably constant during Phase 2.

However, the graphs show a twenty to thirty per cent drop, by tonnage, in conventional trade on pre-Phase 2 averages. This loss of trade must affect the port's overall viability and hence requires some explanation. If it is not due to movements in labour productivity—and hence to movements in costs *since* Phase 2—the explanation might be that costs were initially pitched too high. The movement of PLA rates and charges is relevant at this point. In September 1970 the PLA raised its charges by $17\frac{1}{2}$ per cent, but this proved not to cover the increased costs of Phase 2, so by March 1971 they felt the need to raise charges again by seventy per cent on imports and ninety-one per cent on exports.

[1] *The Port*, 22 October 1970. Later figures suggested that seventy per cent of the loss in conventional trade was made up for in increased mechanized trade.

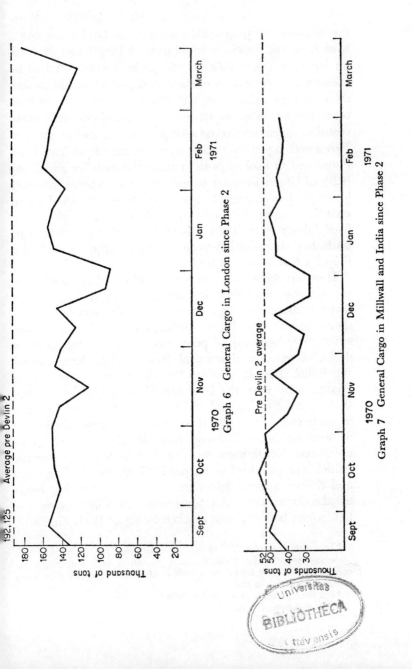

Graph 6   General Cargo in London since Phase 2

Graph 7   General Cargo in Millwall and India since Phase 2

The main reason for this appears to be as follows. With the abolition of piecework, labour costs (and other costs) were fixed and lower tonnages were no longer compensated for by lower costs. To meet the problem the PLA had to raise their revenue from existing trade, which meant raising their charges, even though this in turn was likely to lead to a further drop in trade.[1] The stevedores with their cost-plus system needed no such periodic increase in charges. Faced with a general decline in trade, stevedores have been disinclined to take steps to increase the mobility and flexibility of labour in order to reduce the man-hours involved in cargo movements. Instead they have employed more men than required in order to get the shipper to cover their fixed labour costs. Thus it is probable that the decline in trade has also raised stevedore costs to shippers, with the risk of a further loss in trade.

How did this vicious circle start? If the above analysis is correct, the initial drop in average weekly tonnage in the first few months of the scheme was crucial, especially since these figures were highly publicized as evidence of the scheme's failure and of poor productivity in the London docks.[2] Cyclical and seasonal factors might have caused the initial drop in tonnage but there were other causes. Firstly, there were the increased charges to shippers; the PLA increase in September 1970 was their second increase in six months. Secondly, there was the lack of coincidence of working hours between two-shift dockers and traditional one-shift lightermen. This limited receiving overside (which was one-third of all pre-1967 imports in London)[3], and deliveries from lighterage craft, to the working hours of the lightermen. An agreement on shiftworking for lightermen had not been reached by April 1971. Similarly,

---

[1] In expectation of a further drop in trade, the PLA March increases were said to be higher than necessary to restore its profit margin on existing trade. They contained a built-in element of compensation for a prospective decline in trade.

[2] e.g. *Sunday Times*, 29 November 1970.

[3] *Annual Reports* of PLA.

lorry drivers have not been on double shifts and thus have not always spread their arrivals and departures within the full span of the 7 a.m.–9 p.m. day; the first seven weeks of the Phase 2 scheme saw a nine per cent drop in vehicles unloaded despite the longer working day. Thirdly, there was the go-slow over 'con' payments for fork-lift truck drivers which lasted in parts of the London docks for up to a month. Fourthly, some employers found the transfer of ships less flexible than the transfer of labour previously used to maintain full working. Finally, there was the shift to mechanized cargo handling, not included in the figures.

In a trade as seasonal and cyclical as port operations, a temporary drop in trade for seven weeks would not normally have caused alarm. Most of the special factors listed above could be considered temporary. The publicity given to these first seven weeks' figures, however, and the evidence they were supposed to afford of the failure of Devlin, may well have discouraged shipping companies from using London and helped to make the drop in trade permanent. Firm B showed a dramatic improvement in its throughput and efficiency between 1967 and 1970,[1] yet, at a press conference in March 1971, it blamed the bad publicity that the port of London had received since Phase 2, especially from the BBC television documentary 'Ports in Peril', for its difficulties in attracting new trade. If bad publicity helped to make the initial drop in tonnage permanent, then the increased charges which were stimulated by this drop[2] further assisted the decline.[3]

It is thus impossible to say whether the effort of dockers dropped with the abolition of piecework and, if it did,

---

[1] See Chapter 16.

[2] It may be that this decline in trade is not unwelcome to all employers. It has been the occasion for the PLA to announce plans to close many of its older and less well-paying berths in the remaining three sectors and to concentrate on its mechanized and modern berths.

[3] As evidence of the self-reinforcing effects of a drop in tonnage the graph on the Millwall and India sector shows that tonnage was up in the first two months of Phase 2 and then declined in line with port figures of weekly tonnages.

whether such a drop in effort was compensated by an improved organization of work in the port generally. There are no port productivity figures to justify a conclusion on either of these questions. Some commentators have used the published figures on the drop in trade outside mechanized cargo handling areas to suggest that the dockers' effort has declined, but that is inadequate evidence. If the drop in trade causes the labour force to be underemployed, and if that labour force is on a fixed wage as it is now, then labour costs per ton moved will rise. Also such underemployment may encourage the overmanning of jobs and the maintenance of restrictive working practices. What cannot be shown, however, is that the drop in trade was due to the abolition of piecework.

16

The 1967 Agreement

Previous sections have described the effects of Phase 1 and Phase 2 on two firms affected by the national and port negotiations on the Devlin Committee's recommendations. This section will explore the experiences of a third firm, Firm B, as it moved independently from casual employment on piecework to permanent employment on a fixed wage in July 1967 and then to two-shift working in July 1969. But since Firm B acted independently and ahead of other port employers, the section also explores how far Firm B acted as a wage leader and pacemaker.

Firm B has always been a relatively independent employer. It is not a member of the National Port Employers' Association or of the LOTEA. It was thus in a position to act independently of other port employers in London, although prior to 1967 its piecework rates were loosely based on those of other employers. It is a relatively small employer and so has not felt constrained, as the PLA clearly has, from acting independently. Unlike traditional stevedores it has always leased the area of the docks in which it did its work rather than simply following ships to where they were assigned.

Technical change provided the incentive to reform. The firm has adopted modern unit-loading techniques which are especially applicable for their Canary Isles fruit trade. These incorporate palletization (the strapping of cargo to pallets which are moved on ship and quay by fork-lift trucks and other mechanized equipment). This necessitated a new type of ship with side-loading as opposed to the traditional hatch-loading. New berths had to be built in the Millwall part of the dock with wide quays, large open sheds for quick transit rather than storage, and wide areas for lorry transport.

In its press conference in March 1971 the firm claimed it had invested over three million pounds in its operation at Millwall docks including over three hundred thousand pounds in sheds and quay equipment. As representatives of its men said at that conference, this visible investment was an important factor in building up the trust which the men had in their employer. More immediately this invest-ment in new handling techniques convinced the firm that a casual labour force working a traditional gang-based piecework system was inappropriate. Thus the firm decasualized in July 1967, before the rest of the port.

In July 1967, the firm took on 246 'preference' men[1] as permanent employees, abolished piecework, and offered a guaranteed basic wage of £29 10s (£29.50), high compared with average port earnings of £23 4s 9d (£23.23). Whether this figure was much above average earnings at the firm itself is another question. The fruit trade gave dockers great power in negotiation and it is generally admitted that the regular followers of Firm B were among the most militant in the dock. A member of the firm's works committee in 1969 claimed that the high basic rate meant a drop in actual earnings for him, but that this was made worthwhile by decasualization, security of earnings, and high fringe benefits in sick and holiday pay. In return Firm B hoped to get rid of restrictive labour practices associated with gang piecework systems and to operate a terminal labour force, mobile and flexible between ship and quay and shed, and within each ship and shed. Free manning was to apply. After two years the 1967

---

[1] Under the casual system there were three classes of docker in London: those who were permanently employed on a weekly basis ('perms.'); casuals with first claim on a firm's daily requirements for men ('preference' men); and the rest.

agreement was replaced by another which graded dockers and introduced shiftwork at higher basic rates.

The operation of the 1967 agreement revealed two problems: free manning and flexibility were in conflict with the residual values and practices of a labour force still organized on a group principle and subject to continuing variable elements in its pay; and new methods of supervision were needed to replace the self-regulating piecework system. These problems were of the same type as were to face London port employers generally when they moved from Phase 1 to Phase 2. Restrictions on free manning were associated particularly with overtime but were given shape by the organization of the work force into units.

Daily overtime was the remaining variable in Firm B's payment system after 1967 and was a recurring item in works committee minutes. These recorded several management complaints about 'boxing' for overtime. On one occasion a unit was disciplined for refusing to accept 7 p.m. orders, insisting on a longer period of overtime being offered. There are no figures on the absolute amounts of overtime worked but the earnings figures show that overtime was a regular element in dockers' pay at Firm B.[1] One result of the increase in tonnage after 1967 was a more regular use of overtime than had been intended; this is reflected in the abandonment of the proposed overtime rota, overtime being assigned to those already working on the job. This aroused interest, however, in the distribution of jobs carrying an overtime bonus. The labour office had to keep a check on the number of times a gang was working on those ships which often required overtime.

Overtime disputes were complicated by the organization of the work force. The purpose of the 1967 agreement was to replace the gang system and its associated practices by a terminal labour force, but, for administrative purposes

[1] See Graph 4, p. 30.

of assigning men to work, it was felt necessary to organize the force into units of nine including the appropriate number of specialists. The labour force was divided into twenty units which were placed in a rota and sent out as the superintendent required them. Where larger or smaller teams were required units were broken down (in reverse order) and individuals distributed accordingly. On the task the units were supposed to be flexible and liable to be split up as the foreman required. But the men liked working in stable groups and the unit system helped them to present a united front against pressure from increasingly efficient supervision, and to operate the 'hop' system.[1] Consequently, the units were in conflict with management's original aim of a fully flexible labour force. From 1967 to 1969 there were regular complaints by the management in works committee meetings under the flexibility clause of the 1967 agreement.

The uneven occurrence of overtime and the organization of the work force into increasingly cohesive units generated questions now that overtime was given to those already working on the job. How many of them should be assigned overtime? How long a period on the job entitled a man to the available overtime? If there was to be overtime, the men wanted every docker working on the job to be offered overtime, to avoid discrimination; and they refused to be moved away from their unit during normal hours if overtime was expected.

The first problem is illustrated by a dispute leading to a two-week overtime ban. Overtime orders were given to only one of the two units working a ship. The men refused to accept the orders unless they were given to both units. The men were suspended for three days, and although the penalty was reduced to one day by the Dock Labour Board, there was a ban on overtime.

[1] The 'hop' system enabled men to be temporarily absent from their units.

The second problem led not only to objections from the units to being broken down on the job, but also to objections from men who had been separated from their units to being sent back if there was a prospect of overtime on the new job. Thus it came to be the rule—similar to the old continuity rule—that when a unit was broken down and individuals were assigned to a job for that day, they had to be allocated to the same job on the next day if extra 'make-up' men were still required. One afternoon, for example, four men were separated from their unit and assigned to a job. Next day they were shifted again, and, consequently lost an overtime period of three hours. They claimed payment in lieu of the overtime, and won it by threatening a stoppage.

Another threat to stop work arose over the handling of baggage. Eighteen passengers had disembarked from a ship on a Sunday without a unit being called in to handle their baggage. The unit which would have handled the baggage claimed payment for the Sunday. The management replied that it was a local customs agreement that baggage could be handled by the ship's crew if there were less than twenty-five passengers. The men's representatives on the works committee argued that dockers should handle the passengers' baggage, and the union backed them. The management said that in any case a full unit would not have been needed but they were told there had been no opportunity to see how many men were required. After a series of emergency meetings the whole unit was credited with the appropriate overtime payment, it being left to the men in question to decide either independently or collectively to donate this payment to any charitable organization that they wish to name.[1]

One reason why these conflicts did not lead to strikes at Firm B was the works committee of five representatives of management and five dockers. This meets monthly but can

---

[1] Minutes of Works Committee Meeting 10.1.69.

be summoned for emergency meetings. It acts as a forum for dockers' views on a wide range of subjects, and is not merely a consultative body, but provides an opportunity for the workers' representatives to make their claims on management. Along with full-time union officials, the five members formed a negotiating committee to deal with the 1969 agreement.

With the 1967 agreement, management realized that supervision was a problem. Supervisors acted as individuals rather than a team, and did not see themselves as part of management.[1] To change this situation the firm tried to build a management team by weekly meetings of all managers, including supervisors, for open discussion of current problems. At these meetings, problems were successively defined and solutions introduced or offered; from these solutions 'optimal strategies' were developed.

A sociologist who observed these meetings over a period of fifteen months noted several changes. There was a decline in disagreements between management and supervisors and between supervisors and supervisors. At the beginning the supervisors ranked social skills above decision-making or problem-solving skills, but subsequently reversed this order. For the first year there was a marked increase in the effectiveness of time spent making decisions, and conflicts between supervisors and the men increased over the whole period indicating that supervisors saw things from a manager's rather than a docker's point of view.

Tonnage increased dramatically during the period of the agreement.[2] Mechanization was largely responsible for this in the fruit trade, but Firm B also expanded its general trade, much of which was not mechanized. To achieve this Firm B had to impose requirements on its customers. They

[1] Mr P. Jackson and Mr K. Eagle from Birkbeck College, London, provided much of the information used here from their studies of supervision at this firm.

[2] Between 1967 and 1970 tonnage doubled without any increase in the labour force.

gave preference to palletized cargo for export. The experience of Firm B showed that changes in internal supervision were not enough. They have to be seen as only one aspect of changes in work organization. Changes were also required of customers in their habits and attitudes to the use of dock facilities.

17

The 1969 Agreement

The problems thrown up by the first agreement were associated with units and overtime. The works committee agreed that units had become 'clannish' and were competing for earnings. The 1969 agreement, therefore, abolished units and put an end to daily overtime by introducing shift-work, although overtime work on Sunday remained. The men were divided into two grades—Grade 1 being fit for all work and Grade 2 for quay work only—and were assigned to work individually.

Compared with the general scheme for the port, Firm B's agreement had the advantages of being tailored to the firm's requirements and of access to a constitutional body, the works committee, which could make amendments where necessary. The works committee interpreted and modified the agreement, recording any changes in their minutes. In genuine cases of late arrival, for example, the committee agreed that a docker should, if possible, be given the chance of working the afternoon shift as an alternative to losing pay. But this alternative was to be available only once every six months, and then only if management had a job for him. The agreement said nothing about recruitment. Hence the works committee negotiated specific arrangements when the firm decided to recruit seventeen more men to allow for the dockers' preference for near relatives over 'outsiders'.

In addition to works committee meetings, Firm B's manager meets the men at group meetings. During the first agreement he had tried to start unit meetings to discuss company policy with the men, but they were abandoned as divisive. Under the second agreement the manager has begun to hold group meetings on the morning shift. When the work allows, groups of ten to fifteen men come for informal discussions with him. Originally he wanted to test their feelings, but now the meetings are used to explain policies more fully than is done by works committee minutes. The workers' side of the works committee favours these meetings as 'verbal suggestion boxes' and does not feel that they undermine its own position.

How does the 1969 agreement deal with the problems raised by the first agreement? The abolition of daily overtime has ended boxing and other overtime disputes and the abolition of units has lessened opposition to free manning. But the firm still has to satisfy the men's concern for fair shares. Specific rotas for work on loose bags, which used to be hard work, have now gone because the firm has demanded of its customers that such bags be pre-slung for mechanized discharge, and working conditions are now 'near enough the same' on all ships, according to workers' representatives. But men still demand that 'perks' of time-off, overtime on Sundays, and 'cons' for crane driving are fairly distributed.

Time off due to lack of work can occur in two forms. Firstly, the firm's workload may not require every man who is due in on that shift. This means that some men get a day off. It can be foreseen, and men are informed on the previous day that they will not be required. These days off are shared equally throughout the labour force. Since they are governed by fluctuations in work they cannot be shared in strict rotation, but no individual can have a second day off before everybody has had a first day off.

Secondly, time off can occur through early finishes due to shortage of work. This does not appear to be common at Firm B. The work force is split 2:1 between the morning and afternoon shifts. This means the bulk of work is done in the morning, while the afternoon shift works essential holds and does preparatory work for the following day.

Consequently, early finishes are more likely to occur in the morning shift when men are less concerned with finishing early. Perhaps this is the reason why there appears to be no pressure for early finishes at Firm B. Workers seem to be confident that serious shortages of work will give some of them a whole shift off and that these days will be shared equally.

The possessive attitude towards jobs which was associated with units and daily overtime in the 1967 agreement is no longer evident. There is no formal rotation of early finishes when they do occur, and no pressure to spread early finishes to the whole working group. Men used to working together know whose turn it is for an early finish; otherwise they simply toss a coin.

The only additional payment or con generally available at Firm B is for crane driving. The labour superintendent said that many men felt it should have been abolished under the second agreement but management had wanted to retain it to make sure that men would volunteer for the work. No rota is required since there is a shortage of crane drivers. Winch driving is considered more boring, as well as colder in winter, than crane driving and there has been some pressure for cons for winch driving. The workers' side of the works committee are reserving their position here until the July 1971 review of the agreement. They do insist, however, that crane driving jobs which carry a con should be available only to those who are able and willing to drive winches.

There is no pressure to extend con payments to other specialists such as the top men, who co-ordinate work on ship or quay and are paid as gangers elsewhere, or to fork-lift truck drivers (although their claim for a con under Phase 2 led to a work to rule elsewhere). Apart from the con for crane driving Firm B's men seem to think that all of them should be paid the same rate. Almost all of them (about ninety-five per cent) drive fork-lift trucks so that a con for this work would constitute a wage increase for the whole firm. They feel that the proper place and time to negotiate this is the revision of the firm's agreement every two years.

The third source of variation is Sunday overtime which is covered by strict rotas, one for Grade 1 and another for Grade 2. The workers' representatives say that if overtime is wanted only aboard ship, they insist that overtime is equalized by bringing in only Grade 2 men as soon as future overtime occurs on the quay. They have also decided to work without safety officers on Sunday. Normally the presence of safety officers, who are dockers who have attended special courses, is required. As there are not many of them they got more Sunday overtime than the rest until the workers' representatives insisted that Sunday work no longer required their presence.

On the same principle of equality of opportunity, offers of specialist training have to be available generally, not just to selected men. Vacant jobs were offered to relatives, as long as they satisfied the firm's skill requirements, on the principle of 'one bite of the cherry'. The family of each docker at the firm had one offer of a recruitment interview in turn until all the families at the firm had had an offer.

Consequently, although norms of equality and solidarity remain, they do not lead to the same type of conflict with management over work methods or pay as during the 1967 agreement or under piecework. This is not to say that issues of pay or manning have been finally settled. When the review comes up, the dockers at Firm B will be making a pay claim to restore their differential over other port workers, and manning problems remain latent. Workers' representatives feel that manning is barely adequate, but they are ready to press for recruitment if trade increases.

The atmosphere at Firm B is impressive. Specific complaints and conflicts of interest arise, but they are subject to constitutional settlement; and there appears to be a general commitment to the experiment in which the firm feels it is engaged. Managers are satisfied that foremen share management aims, although the foremen still belong to the T&G and make claims through the union. Workers talk of trusting the firm and management think labour's performance has been 'terrific.'

18

Firm B and Other Port Workers

Firm B acted independently and defined its objectives to suit its own needs. Its employees have remained aloof from what they consider to be the domestic affairs of dockers at other firms. They refused to take part in the work-to-rule over additional payments for forklift truck drivers in September and October 1970, and they have not involved themselves in strikes at the other firms. But neither management nor workers are indifferent to what is happening elsewhere in the London docks.

The dockers are members of the T&G and enjoy unusually good relations with their full-time officer. One of Firm B's dockers is a member of the divisional committee[1] of the union. The men supported the official national dock strike of July 1970 and the December 1970 strike over the Industrial Relations Bill as directed by the No. 1 Docks Group. The second strike over the Bill in January 1971 was not endorsed by No. 1 Docks Group and therefore not observed.

Firm B's dockers are not indifferent to what is paid elsewhere. After the Pearson report in July 1970 they demanded a general increase of £1 a week which they felt was justified by the settlement of the national strike. The amount of their claim for additional shift payments for crane drivers was based on a comparison with the cons paid to these specialists at other firms. In the review of their agreements in July 1971 the workers' representatives propose to restore their differential over other port workers which was eroded by the Phase 2 settlement, and to

[1] See Appendix III

demand a fourth week's paid holiday now that port workers elsewhere in London have three weeks paid holiday.

For their part Firm B's agreements have been important reference points for dockers elsewhere in London and in the Millwall and India sector in particular. Chapter 4 showed that Firm B was a wage leader in the Millwall and India sector and that average earnings in other firms followed earnings at Firm B during Phase 1 of Devlin. Its 1969 agreement became an important yardstick for subsequent negotiations for Phase 2 in the port as a whole. *The Port*[1] saw it as a 'pathmaker', and it embarrassed both unions and employers. T&G members criticized their union for signing a separate agreement with one firm alone while port negotiations were in progress. Union officials at the Royals and Millwall and India docks were asked how they could expect men in the port generally to accept a wage structure of £25 to £36 a week when the Firm B agreement gave £39 a week. At the end of 1970 *The Port* commented that the union's attitude 'very much reflects that of the men in the docks who by now regard (Firm B's) agreement as the yardstick'.

Similarly other port employers were clearly embarrassed by the 1969 agreement of Firm B which was more favourable than their own current offers. They were reported in *The Port* in September 1969 as being very much aware that if they were able to offer the same conditions that have been offered at (Firm B's) berth at Millwall they could get immediate agreement, but as unable to do so for three reasons: Firm B could channel as many of its ships to its own berths as it wanted, and thus keep them fully employed; the firm had complete mobility of labour; and, more important still, the economics of running a terminal berth were different to those of other port operations. In the event, however, the final settlement of Phase 2 was very close to Firm B's agreement of July 1969.

---

[1] *The Port* newspaper is one of the most important organs of opinion in the London docks. It has a circulation of 18,000 mostly in London, and its coverage is mainly of London dock affairs.

19

Multi-Unionism

Previous sections have dealt only in passing with the part played by unions and union officials. The Devlin Committee, in fact, identified two deficiencies in union organization which were detrimental to industrial relations in the docks: multi-unionism and inter-union conflict, and poor internal union communications. Developments in these two areas since decasualization will now be examined. This chapter looks first at the problems that arise from multi-unionism in the London docks.

There are two unions in the enclosed docks in London for the same types of dock worker; NASDU (the stevedores' or 'blue' union) and the T&G (the dockers' or 'white' union). These had closed shops prior to decasualization and an agreement between them specified each union's sphere of influence and exclusive job rights. While these arrangements were apparently fixed, changes in trade made them unstable. When Firm B moved from Canary Wharf, South West India Dock to their new berth in Millwall in 1966, taking their regular dockers (T&G members) with them, stevedores (NASDU members) felt this was a breach of traditional inter-union arrangements.[1] A serious demarcation dispute resulted which led to a Court of Inquiry under Sir Roy Wilson.

The strike highlighted one problem of multi-unionism

[1] These arrangements gave NASDU control of all shipwork in the Millwall docks and exporting shipwork in the India docks. Firm B had been an exception, even in there, since all its work including exporting shipwork was done by T & G dockers.

in the London docks, namely inter-union conflict associated with job demarcation. Demarcation disputes of this sort have been rare and none have occurred since 1966, although blue union members in Millwall object to the expansion of Firm B's operations there. The Wilson report in 1966 showed that the fundamental cause of that particular dispute was the decline of dock work in London and the consequent fear of redundancy. Multi-unionism gave a focus to this fear, but it can also find expression within a single union. Apart from the NASDU stewards at Firm A, the T&G stewards at the PLA resented Firm B's agreements because they were taking work away from their members, though the workers at Firm B also belonged to the T&G.

The Wilson Court of Inquiry said that a common register for similarly qualified members of both unions would put an end to demarcation disputes. In fact, there were no separate registers for dockers and stevedores under the casual system but members of the two unions were distinguishable by their registration numbers. Using this differentiation stevedores were offered only 'stevedore work' and dockers 'docker work' according to the union's arrangements dividing up the London docks. Since decasualization there has been a common register which means that individual stevedores or dockers can work wherever they are assigned; they are assigned without reference to any exclusive rights as the unions no longer claim them. However, the previous division of the port into areas of jurisdiction reflected the distribution of union membership in the port. With decasualization, stevedores and dockers were assigned to the employers who regularly employed them and so the division of work between stevedores and dockers continued. NASDU members still work mainly for private stevedores, and T&G members still work for the quay employer (i.e. the PLA) and such ship employers as they had worked for prior to the common register, i.e. the PLA on discharge in the India docks and private stevedores in the Royals and Tilbury. Despite a common register decasualization has

E

largely fossilized the previous inter-union arrangements by preventing the free movement of men between jobs.

The Wilson Court of Inquiry also criticized multi-unionism and the lack of a common register for preventing the individual member of each union from having a free choice of work. It said many men would be bound to suffer frustration if their capabilities could not be fully utilized or they were denied the opportunity of a less arduous job when afflicted with age or infirmity. This lack of freedom of choice still causes frustration. But it is no longer caused by multi-unionism and the lack of a common register. It is now due to the division between ship and quay employers. Even during Phase 1 the temporary transfer of labour only rarely allowed a wider choice of jobs to the dockers or stevedores involved. Stevedores at Firm A, for example, complained that blue union men were not treated fairly when lent to predominantly white union firms. But they were not the only dockers to complain. It seems that no borrowed employees received the same treatment in the allocation of the best jobs as the borrowing firm's own employees. Since stevedores were known to be equipped for shipwork, borrowed stevedores were assigned to this more arduous work even by the employers who did both ship and quay work. The view of one union official was that despite a common register, work allocation lacked selectivity, i.e. the placement of individuals in the jobs most suitable to their age, strength, and abilities. Since Phase 2 no transfer of labour is allowed so that dockers and stevedores are more immobile than ever between different types of work.

Multi-unionism may cause competition for members and disputes about 'poaching'. There was trouble of this type between NASDU and the T&G in Liverpool and in Hull in the 1950s, which began when NASDU started to recruit at the expense of the T&G. In London in contrast NASDU and the T&G are both well established, with mutually agreed spheres of influence which have prevented poaching. This sphere of influence agreement was voided when the unions accepted the common register, so they signed a new agreement permitting the free transfer of members between them. It has not led to efforts by either union to attract members from the other though it does appear to have led to some transfer of members from NASDU to the T&G. This might reflect, as a T&G officer claimed, the superior service that the larger union can give its members, but other reasons emerged in the course of this study. Transfers were encouraged at the PLA because the shop stewards and union officers were from the T&G, which was the predominant union there. Also during Phase 1, one night a month, termed 'bath-night' was set aside at the PLA for T&G branch meetings, whereas attendance at NASDU branch meetings might involve loss of overtime pay. At Firm A, where the predominant union was NASDU, the reason for the transfer of two gangs to the T&G was that their future employment prospects in other firms, particularly Firm B, would be better if they became T&G members. But whatever the shifts in membership between the two unions and the reasons for them, there is no poaching in London, nor has there been in recent memory.

Multi-unionism can also cause confusion in collective bargaining either by dual representation at the work-floor level or by union competition or policy differences in formal negotiations. Fear of dual representation and the confusion it might cause was the reason given by workers' representatives at Firm B for insisting that only members of the T&G be employed at the firm. In fact, at the other firms studied dual unionism does not appear to cause representational problems, probably because in both of them one union has an overwhelming majority of members. At Firm A the great majority (ninety per cent) are NASDU members. Since decasualization all the stewards there have been NASDU members, and this appears to be accepted by T&G members. Full-time officers from either union may operate there when a dispute involving mixed gangs occurs, but in fact, NASDU officers were generally used (in particular their 'outdoor' officer) without complaint by the T&G minority in the firm.

At the PLA, the situation is reversed with the great majority of dockers being T&G members and only a minority belonging to NASDU. All PLA stewards, except one, have been from the T&G and the full-time officers involved in disputes since decasualization have been T&G officers. Again this appears to be accepted by the NASDU minority. However, a NASDU member was elected as a shop steward for the Millwall Department in 1970. He had previously been a steward for an area of the department whose labour force was not involved in the general allocation of work at Millwall. It was an enclave of NASDU membership in the department which has now ceased to exist. As a NASDU member this steward says he contacts his own union officer with problems rather than T&G officers, because he finds the latter less accessible. He says that his constituents, the majority of whom are T&G members, do not resent either this practice or his membership of NASDU.

Dual representation does not appear to have caused any great problems, but there is reason to believe that the existence of two unions instead of one complicated the Phase 2 negotiations. T&G officials complained early on in the negotiations that the different negotiating principles of NASDU, particularly the latter's continual reference back to lay members for approval, were delaying negotiations. In April 1969 a general meeting of 4,000 NASDU members rejected any agreement involving shiftwork. The different policies of the two unions were apparent, and NASDU negotiators left the Enclosed Docks Modernization Committee which was negotiating Phase 2. This appears to illustrate the point that multi-unionism can impede collective bargaining. But the evidence is deceptive and the existence of two unions may even have expedited the Phase 2 negotiations. The T&G continued to negotiate Phase 2 after NASDU left the committee and at the second attempt in April 1970 persuaded its members to vote for the employers' offer. The majority in favour was 2,300 in a poll of about sixty per cent. Subsequently

NASDU members removed their ban on shiftwork and authorized their officers to re-open negotiations. As the minority union in the docks, their members undoubtedly felt some need to fall in line with the majority union's vote. But NASDU officials were also concerned that they would lose to the T&G those of their members who favoured the new shiftwork agreement. NASDU, thus attached itself to the final agreement on Phase 2. But it is certain that the NASDU stand against shiftwork and their objections to other aspects of the employers' offers were shared by many T&G members, and it is possible that if there had been a vote of all dockers (both T&G and NASDU members) the April 1970 offer would have been rejected. As well as offering evidence of the delay multi-unionism can bring to collective bargaining the Phase 2 negotiations also offer evidence of the scope given to employers to divide and rule.

20

Internal Union Communications

Union Policy
Multi-unionism was one of two problems of union organization cited by the Devlin Committee. The other was poor communication between full-time officers and lay members. This latter criticism was levelled particularly against the T&G which was said to be out of touch with its members, with the result that the docks had experienced an abnormally high amount of unofficial activity and had thrown up unofficial groups like the Port Liaison Committee. The Devlin Committee recommended that the T&G organize a great campaign to show its members that it had a sound policy and the means for carrying it out. It was further hoped that the development of a shop steward system would improve contacts between lay members and union officials.

Decasualization immediately gave rise to large-scale strikes in London and Liverpool which indicated how much the union had lost touch with its members. The London strike, which cost a quarter of a million working days, crystallized around the continuity rule. There was confusion as to how decasualization arrangements would affect continuity work and then, when these were clarified, some dockers objected to the arrangements for the return of borrowed men to their own employers before they had completed continuity jobs. The T&G had failed to point out to its members how decasualization would affect traditional working practices or to get its members' approval for the changes.

The great campaign to publicise its policy and win back the active co-operation of its members recommended by the Devlin Committee has not taken place. But the Phase 2 negotiations saw a greater involvement of lay members than had occurred before. The elected committees of the dockers, i.e. the PLA Lay Committee, the Ocean Trade Lay Committee (for private stevedoring employment) and the No. 1 Docks Group[1] were not new, and they had previously supplied members of port negotiating bodies. However, the Phase 2 negotiations showed these lay members to be in a dominating position in union policy in the negotiations. Firstly, in addition to their representation on the Enclosed Docks Modernization Committee they composed the *majority* of the union side in the crucial sub-committee that sat in the second half of 1969. Secondly, the negotiators continually referred back to the three lay committees (PLA Lay Committee, Ocean Trade Lay Committee and No. 1 Docks Group) and twice to the conference of dock delegates. Thirdly, and most important, the No. 1 Docks Group imposed the container ban forbidding any further local agreements on mechanized working from January 1968 until Phase 2 had been negotiated. This ban was of fundamental importance in giving urgency to the negotiations because of the delay involved to Overseas Containers Limited's new container terminal. This ban was not maintained without difficulty; one vote of No. 1 Docks Group gave only a six to five majority in favour of continuation. But it originated and was maintained by the lay committee of the union in London against the advice of the union officers. Finally, the decision of lay representatives to recommend acceptance of the employers' offer in April was probably crucial in persuading the members to reverse their vote against acceptance.

All the same the T&G was still criticized for its conduct of negotiations. Members of both the T&G and NASDU felt that the T&G, in contrast to NASDU, did not keep its

[1] See Appendix III.

members fully informed of the state of the negotiations. To do no more than set out the employers' proposals in a circular before the two votes of the members was thought to be inadequate. This inhibited worthwhile discussion at the general meetings prior to the votes and made the results of the ballots less meaningful. Full-time officers might feel that these criticisms should be levelled at lay committee members who were supposed to act as a two-way channel of communication. Not all of these lay members held mass meetings to ensure the continued support of the lay committee policies, as was done at Tilbury. It is difficult to see what the union could have done except to hold more mass meetings. More progress reports on the state of negotiations might have been circulated but the fortnightly *Port* newspaper was already providing adequate accounts.

Lay participation was, then, an important aspect of the Phase 2 negotiations. It may also have been one reason why in London Phase 2 was introduced without the strikes that accompanied the introduction of Phase 1. Full-time union officers of the T&G may not, however, have accepted this new degree of lay participation from choice. The district officer interviewed still made a distinction between the T&G and the NASDU in this respect. He felt a union officer should lead and formulate opinion, not follow every temporary whim of the membership. He should therefore have the power to settle in negotiations and not to be continually referring back to members like the NASDU officers.

Shop Stewards and Full-Time Union Officers

One reason why the Phase 2 negotiations exhibited a greater degree of lay participation may have been the widespread development of a shop steward system for the London docks following the Devlin Committee's recommendations. In fact shop stewards were not a novel feature everywhere in the docks. The PLA had worker representatives before decasualization. In the departments studied they simply carried on as before under the new title of shop stewards.

However, shop stewards were an innovation for private stevedores. Their negotiating functions had previously been carried out by gang representatives or unofficial bodies like the Port Liaison Committee in the Royals.

The experience of the Royals justified the Devlin Committee's belief that unofficial groups ('the wreckers') existed only because there was no formal, constitutional shop steward system. According to a leading member of the Port Liaison Committee, the committee revived in 1968 only because of the failure of the shop steward system to 'get off the ground' in the Royals. When agreement was finally reached with the employers on the number of full-time shop stewards in 1969, Jack Dash put the committee, in his words, 'into cold storage'. Indeed the desire of some of the leading members of the committee 'to go official' by becoming divisional union representatives might otherwise have been embarrassing.

But if the shop steward system has proved an alternative to unofficial groups, how far have stewards been integrated into the union structure and what has been the relationship between full-time union officers and shop stewards? Certainly shop stewards in the docks, as elsewhere, provide important services for the union like the quarterly checking of union cards. But the relationship between stewards and union officials has not been universally happy. In studying the operation of Phase 1 it was noticed that T&G stewards at the PLA objected to outside interference, as they termed it, from the full-time union officers in the day-to-day negotiations in their departments. In particular they objected to piecework disputes being referred for resolution to the PLA Group Joint Committee where union officers would represent the men's case. It seemed to the stewards that such committees rarely supported their case and they ascribed this to the fact that only one of the five workers' representatives was a lay member. They felt that full-time union officers were unaware of changing conditions in the docks and insensitive to the informal rules and working methods peculiar to each department and even each shed.

Full-time officers denied this charge, but there was a marked preference on the part of PLA stewards for settling issues in the department without involving union officers.

At Firm A, by contrast, there was no such resentment of outside union officers of NASDU. This was ascribed by the stewards to a difference between NASDU and the T&G in the accessibility and sympathy of full-time officers. But stewards were new to Firm A in Phase 1 and they might be expected to rely more on the union officers. Moreover, disputes at Firm A did not go outside the firm to the Ocean Trades Group Joint Committee so that when union officials were involved it was in discussion with the firm.

At Firm B the relationship between T&G officers and workers' representatives was much more amicable than the relationship between the same officers and PLA representatives. Workers' representatives were left to settle day to day issues through the works committee, with union officials being brought in on especially intractable problems and on the biennial re-negotiation of the basic agreement at the firm. Full-time officers were happy with their restricted role at Firm B; and the workers' representatives appreciated their help.

The crucial factor determining the relationship between union officers and shop stewards in Phase 1 seems to have been the payment system. Day to day piecework bargaining resulted in highly informal, fragmented and often *ad hoc* settlements. Where stewards had been involved in this bargaining for some time, they felt, rightly or wrongly, that full-time officers were insensitive to the arrangements with which they were dealing. At Firm B the greater formality of agreements and collective bargaining and the smaller number of disputes led to a more congenial relationship developing between union officers and workers' representatives at the firm.

If this is true then it might be expected that relationships between full-time officers and stewards would have improved after Phase 2 abolished piecework. In fact, at the PLA the relationship between the stewards and their officers appears to be worse in one respect. Previously, an officer of the general workers' trade group had serviced certain groups of ancillary workers around the dock but, the group having been abolished, this officer's duties are now shared out by dockers' officers. PLA stewards say this has made officers even more inaccessible and out of touch. The one PLA steward who is a NASDU member says that this is the reason he contacts his own union officer rather than the T&G officer. PLA stewards said that when they were able to contact T&G officers, they did not get very much help on the issues they brought to them; the officers left it to the stewards to interpret the agreement, saying, just as management did, that: 'It's all in the Green Book'. There is a provision in the Green Book for the attendance of full-time officers at the stewards' meetings with docks managers but the opportunity was not generally taken up. According to the stewards, T&G officers have attended only two of these meetings. These were over the work-to-rule, 'funnily enough', as one steward caustically remarked.

Stewards at Firm A retain daily contact with their NASDU officer and shared the feeling of their predecessors that their officers were more accessible than T&G officers and that their union had greater lay control. Firm B continue to enjoy a better relationship between the works committee and T&G officers than exists between the PLA stewards and their officers. One reason for this is that Firm B's agreements have been publicized as copybook agreements and the union officer is proud of them and strongly committed to them.

The policy of the T&G union officers interviewed was to involve shop stewards more fully in the union by encouraging them to stand for election to office in the branches and in the division. One out of eight T&G stewards interviewed was a branch officer and two were divisional representatives. But they seemed to be alone in taking an active part in branch and divisional affairs. Those stewards who were not already branch or divisional representatives expressed no desire to take on these extra duties. In any case branch life was, by common agreement, quiescent during Phase 1. There have been no branch meetings since Phase 2 because there has been no agreement with employers on when these could be arranged under the new two-shift system.

The stewards interviewed at Firm A also avoided branch office, though one former steward subsequently became an executive member of NASDU. They also had no active branch life during Phase 1 and meetings became impossible to arrange after Phase 2.

The normal pattern of involvement of stewards in union policy is not through their branches and divisions but through membership of lay committees. The senior steward at the PLA felt strongly that these committees should be composed of shop stewards who were responsible to their constituents and not of other members who were 'irresponsible'. This view has a good deal in common with the officers' desire to involve shop stewards in branch and divisional life and so make them responsible for carrying out union policy at the workshop level. But, as the Phase 2 negotiations showed, the lay committees and full-time union officers do not necessarily agree on policy.

In its recommendations to the T&G the Devlin Committee seems to have had a rather too simple view of the problem and to have expected too much from the main changes it proposed. It saw poor internal union communications as the T&G's central deficiency and thought this could be changed by a publicity campaign led by union officers. In retrospect it seems fanciful to recommend a great campaign by the T&G to win back the support of its members. There was nothing in recent T&G history in the docks to give any confidence that such a campaign might take place or that, if it did, it would have much effect. Poor internal union communications were not a result of inadequate publicity resources. And the Devlin report itself said deficient communication was not due to a shortage of full-time officers. It was rather a result of disagreement between union officers and members over policy, together with the exclusion of full-time officers from daily negotiations on pay and work. In practice full-time officers were excluded from the informal system for dealing with pay which increased in importance in the docks, a process which the Donovan Commission noted in other industries.[1] The union often appeared to its members to be either wrong or irrelevant.

Given this situation, the second major recommendation of the Devlin Committee for improving internal union communications—namely the introduction of a shop steward system—was based on over-optimistic expectations. The Committee's report itself had noted that shop stewards were not unknown in the docks, but presented no evidence to show that union communications before decasualization were any better in firms with stewards than in those without them. During Phase 1 shop stewards in London were still operating a highly informal system of pay and work regulation. Experienced stewards resented what they considered to be the 'outside interference' of union officers in this system. At best, stewards thought that such piecemeal interference was insensitive to informal arrangements. At worst, since it occurred at the request of management and often involved negotiations with senior managers whom the stewards themselves did not usually meet, this interference of union officers marked them off in some steward's eyes as 'employers' men'.

Phase 2 has put an end to the informal system associated with piecework in London. But questions of job allocation, working methods and productivity measurement have arisen under the Phase 2 agreement. In these the T&G stewards have not received the advice they need from their officers. More particularly, the position of full-time shop stewards itself is now insecure. The abolition of piecework has removed the steward's daily negotiating role and employers have expressed the opinion that full-time stewards are not required. Stewards will not accept this

[1] Royal Commission on Trade Unions and Employers' Associations, *Report* 1968, Cmnd. 3623.

contention so long as many questions associated with productivity remain unanswered and have not been negotiated. But their officers have not given them specific support on this issue.

In both Phase 1 and Phase 2 the relationship of the stewards and their union officers has not been universally amicable. The reason is that there has been no clear agreement between employers and unions (both officers and stewards) on the role stewards are to play in collective bargaining. The Phase 2 agreement specified the condition for affording stewards recognition and the procedures available to them for bringing up issues. It did not say what issues they could bring up. One remedy to the present arrangement, which all parties find unsatisfactory, would be the active existence of company and sector productivity committees to analyse and take action upon productivity figures. If such meetings were regular (e.g. monthly) and authoritative, lay participation in them might be exchanged for the present system of full-time shop stewards. Firm B is an example of one firm where workers feel happy to have representatives who are part of the regular work force, and these representatives also have a better working relationship with their T&G officers because both know and agree upon their respective roles. Problems arising at the firm are dealt with by the lay representatives through the firm's works committee. The full-time officer only involves himself in the biennial negotiations on their basic agreement. Even here his role is a supporting one.

In so far as improved internal union communications depend upon a good working relationship between full-time union officers and lay representatives of the union at the workplace, such a relationship is possible only where all the parties—employers, union officers, lay representatives and men—agree on the role of the lay representatives. This role itself is determined not by the policies of the union as much as by those of the employers. It is the importance of the works committee in Firm B which determines and defines the lay representatives' functions there.

Thus if the internal union communications of the T&G remain deficient after the implementation of the Devlin Committee's recommendations, at least part of the responsibility for this must lie with the employers. The Devlin Committee appears to have been optimistic in thinking that the union would change its policy on its own initiative and in believing that the creation of a shop steward system would, in itself, solve the problem of poor internal union communications in the T&G. A system of lay representation at the workplace certainly *can* improve these communications, but the extent to which it does so depends not so much on the use the union makes of such a system, as on what employers make of it.

21

Conclusion

A study of the outcome of the Devlin Committee's recommendations should end with some assessment of their success or failure, but the limits of the evidence are obvious. This is only a study of one part of one port. The Phase 2 schemes that have been introduced in ports outside London, such as Bristol, have differed significantly from the Phase 2 agreements in London, and the results are said to be different. The Devlin report did not specify any particular Phase 2 agreement for any port. It did not say, for example, that pay incentive schemes should be retained as in Bristol, or abolished as in London. The responsibility for the particular post-Devlin schemes rests, as the report said it must, with the parties—unions, employers and dockers in each port.

To be fair to the Devlin Committee, their criteria should be used. They found labour relations in the docks deficient on two grounds: high strike incidence and restrictive work practices. In London, despite decasualization, labour relations did not improve under either heading during Phase 1. In so far as the Devlin Committee attributed poor labour relations in the docks to the casual system itself they were proved wrong. Indeed, judged by a third criterion used by employers, wage drift, labour relations became worse.

By contrast, Phase 2 has diminished the number of strikes—in fact only one strike of Millwall and India dockers was recorded between September 1970 and April 1971. In addition port-wide restrictive practices, such as the continuity rule and general rules on the manning levels of jobs, have ceased to operate. The ability of individual employers to achieve full flexibility and mobility of labour has differed, but the failure of any individual firm in this respect has depended on its degree of mechanization, level of trade, and pricing system rather than on any union policy. Thus, in so far as the Devlin Committee defined the labour problems of the docks as strike-proneness and restrictive practices, and recommended decasualization to bring about a change in payment systems as the means of resolving these problems, they have been proved right.

There is, however, another criterion by which the Devlin Committee recommendations must be judged, namely productivity. Restrictive work practices were condemned because they checked efficiency and reduced productivity. Moreover, the Committee saw that the costs of permanent employment could be met only by removing restrictive practices and improving productivity. Although these practices have gone with Phase 2, productivity is still generally considered to be low, and for this reason the Devlin Committee has been judged by some critics to be a failure. The critics, however, are on weak ground in asserting that abandoning piecework has caused a decline in productivity when no figures on productivity for earlier periods (including Phase 1) are available to allow comparison with Phase 2. The published figures show only that *trade* has declined in the conventional berths of London and that costs have risen. With a permanent labour force on fixed wages, a decline in trade will necessarily cause an increase in labour costs per ton moved. If labour costs per ton are the measure of productivity, then it follows that a decline in trade will cause a decline in productivity. This much seems logically unobjectionable. It cannot be argued, without more evidence, that a decline in productivity, i.e. an increase in labour costs per ton since Phase 2, is causing a decline in trade. The loss of trade may mean that the substantially increased labour costs involved in Phase 2 *could not* be compensated for by increased labour productivity, but different explanations can be offered to account for the initial decline in conventional trade: the increased charges that accompanied the Phase 2 agreement; a shift in trade from conventional to mechanized handling; the failure of ancillary services to accommodate themselves to the two-shift system; and an untimely work-to-rule. The initial drop continued because some of these factors continued to operate but also because of the adverse publicity it attracted.

Productivity is therefore a difficult criterion to apply. What this study has shown is that employers differ in their ability and readiness to change the working methods and practices of their men. Mechanization helps to explain the differences. The more machines employed in dock work, the greater the incentive for the employer to break down traditional gangs and to make his men mobile between different jobs. This is one reason for the difference between Firm A and Firm B, and, since Phase 2, between the PLA and some private stevedores. Another reason is trade. A busy employer is more prepared to break down gangs and transfer men between jobs than one whose business is slack. This helps to explain the different records of Firm A and the PLA under Phase 2; and Firm B has been able to keep its labour force more fully employed than the private stevedores. A third reason is that history and inclination has fitted some employers for undertaking new initiatives in labour policy and not others. The contracting employers, who used to supply labour to ships when and where required, were ill-equipped to operate post-Devlin schemes in London. Not all of them had the fixed stake in the industry, the managerial experience, or indeed the respect of their men needed to operate successfully without casual employment and piecework. The final reason is the division between quay employers and ship employers in London. Early finishes at the private stevedores led to claims for early finishes at the PLA; and the division prevented full flexibility and mobility of dockers over the whole range of jobs. As a terminal employer, Firm B had a better record on mobility of labour than either the private stevedores or the PLA.

How do these findings reflect upon the Devlin Committee's recommendations? Firstly, there are still too many employers on the docks. In fact the London enclosed docks have twice as many employers as the Devlin Committee recommended, and responsibility for this must lie with employers and the government rather than the Devlin Committee. Secondly, the Devlin report did not go far enough, or at least was not specific enough, on the changes in management techniques which the other recommendations required. It should be clear to port employers that the provision of sufficient work to allow the full utilization of labour is a necessary precondition to changing work methods. The inability of some employers to make this provision under Phase 2 does not encourage confidence that mere exhortations would be effective now. What is required is a further reduction in the number of employers; and the replacement of separate ship and quay employers by terminal employers.

So much for the Devlin Committee's recommendations on port management, but what about their recommendations for changing the attitudes of dockers? The Committee were right in suggesting that the attitudes of dockers were not simply the product of a sentimental attachment to the past, but a rational response to conditions of insecurity and inequity. These conditions had their origin in the casual system, but remained after decasualization because of piecework. This study has shown that the abolition of piecework brought a change in attitudes so that some employers could make radical alterations in the rules on the manning of jobs and the distribution of work. Dockers still insisted on a fair sharing of jobs carrying additional payments, but this was more compatible than the previous rules with management aims on flexibility of labour. Dockers are not willing, however, to accept responsibility for poor productivity without a voice in the way productivity is to be achieved. The measurement of productivity will have to involve a joint review of the figures if these are to be accepted by the dockers. Joint committees set up to measure productivity could provide the means for dockers to share in discussions on the best ways of working. This was not specifically recommended by the Devlin Committee but seems a logical extension of their views.

The Devlin Committee's recommendations for accommodation between NASDU and the T&G were directed mainly at improving the relationship of the two unions outside London where inter-union conflict was most pronounced. But they said that arrangements would have to be made between the two unions in London to accommodate the new shop steward system they envisaged, where stewards would have responsibilities for workers of both unions. As they said, this situation was most common in the Royals sector of the London docks. There would appear to be no inter-union trouble about the jurisdictional rights of shop stewards in the Royals, and no difficulties have been caused by the representation of members of the minority union by shop stewards of the majority union at two of the firms studied, or by the representation of members of the majority union by a shop steward of the minority union. Inter-union relations seem to have been improved by the 'common register' agreement between the two unions which enables members to transfer. Two unions for the same category of worker do not seem to create any problems of job demarcation that are not already imposed on the industry by the division of employers; and the existence of two unions did not so much confuse as expedite port negotiations. The Devlin Committee were right not to over-emphasize the difficulties resulting from multi-unionism in the docks.

The Committee's main recommendation about the unions concentrated on improving the internal communications of the T&G. The T&G did not engage in a great campaign to win back the support of its members, as the Committee wished, but the creation of a shop steward system throughout the port brought the demise of the unofficial groups, as the Committee had suggested it would. On the evidence so far, however, this system has not improved communications between full-time officers and lay members as much as the Committee hoped. It gave new authority to the recognized lay committees in the docks. These occupied a powerful position in port negotiations on Phase 2, not so much through official union policy as because of the eventual acceptance by union officers of the *de facto* power of lay committees. During Phase 1, piecework gave shop stewards an important role in a highly informal system of wage determination. The informality of the system made shop stewards feel that the trade union officers were insensitive to particular piecework claims and were of little or no help in piecework negotiations. Under Phase 2 stewards have felt that their officers are not sufficiently responsive to the range of claims and complaints that have arisen under the agreement, or to the insecurity of the shop steward's own position. Final agreement has not yet been reached either on the number of full-time stewards nor on the scope of their job now that piecework has been abolished.

While the relationship between T&G stewards and their full-time union officers is not yet a completely happy one, the officers have a much better relationship with the lay representatives of the union at Firm B. The difference lies in the clear agreement between the parties on the roles the full-time officers and lay representatives are expected to play there. Lay representatives deal with daily problems and full-time officers are called in when their support is needed and for the firm's biennial re-negotiation of its agreement.

The Devlin Committee's view of internal communications thus appears to have been too simple. A system of accredited lay union representation at the workplace does not necessarily improve communication between members and full-time union officers. In so far as communication with the members depends on a good working relationship between the lay representatives and the full-time union officers, what is needed here is a clear understanding between the union officers and lay representatives about the role each is expected to play. Paradoxically, the responsibility for achieving this situation lies less with the union than with the employer. If the employer and lay representatives agree—as they appear to have done at Firm B—on the issues lay representatives are to deal with and the joint negotiating machinery they are to use, then the relationship between the lay representatives and full-time officers is more easily established.

Under Phase 2, employers believe that there are too many full-time stewards doing nothing. The stewards say that such inactivity as they experience results from their not being given the role they want in joint negotiations on work methods, allocation and productivity. They will not accept the employers' proposals for a reduction in the number of full-time stewards. This disagreement could be resolved by adopting the model of Firm B, where lay representatives are working dockers, but with full facilities to take up individual grievances and engage in regular meetings with management on all the general issues that the work force consider important.

On internal communications, then, as on management in the docks, the Devlin Committee's recommendations were not so much wrong as incomplete. There is little evidence that labour relations are responsible for the unhealthy financial situation of the docks. Even if the costs of implementing the Devlin Committee's recommendations in London have helped to undermine the competitive position of the port, the responsibility for this situation lies not with the Committee but with the parties to industrial relations in the London docks, and in particular the employers. They took five years to negotiate agreements on the Devlin Committee's recommendations, by which time the cost of agreement had risen. Even now they have not exploited all the opportunities for new methods of working created by the settlement.

Appendix I

Dock Operations and Terminology in the Port of London

Most cargo for export arrives by road or rail, and the operation of unloading it is termed 'striking'. Some of it is transported directly to the ship's side, but most is stored in sheds and subsequently taken to the quay for loading. Cargo is generally lifted on board ship by means of cranes or winches. Cranes have struts (jibs) which stand out at an angle from the ground and enable them to slew (swing). Winches are more simple pulley devices without jibs and therefore without the same mobility. A ship's fixed equipment or gear may include deck cranes and winches. Larger cranes are available on the quay which can take heavier loads and reach further. Cranes are generally more complicated machines to drive than winches and crane driving has always been a specialist job. On ship the cargo is loaded into holds. By contrast imports are unloaded from the holds, carried to the quay by crane, stored in sheds and loaded thence on to lorries and railway wagons. Some cargo, however, does not pass over the quay at all, but is delivered to or unloaded from the ship by lighters (barges) using the ship's gear. This method of work is termed overside.

When loaded on ship the cargo is stowed and referred to as stowage. The hold in which cargo is stowed may have enclaves referred to as lockers or cupboards. When cargo is packed in bags, dockers call it bagwork. Items of cargo handled individually are termed loose work or loose bags. But to increase the speed of operations cargo may be unit-loaded. One example of unit-loading is the strapping of a number of items to pallet boards. This work is called palletized and if the strapping occurs away from the dock area, pre-palletized. Pallets are wooden boards suitable for handling by fork-lift trucks. Large bags, however, might slip off these boards and so to load or unload several bags at a time they are bound in a canvas sling, and become pre-slung cargo.

This study is concerned with the operations of the enclosed docks, excluding lighterage and wharfinger work on the private wharves along the riverside which are covered by separate negotiating machinery. In the enclosed docks different stages of the cycle of operations are in many instances undertaken by separate firms. It is common for the shipwork of unloading and loading on board ship to be carried out by one employer, while the quay work of transfer to sheds and to inland transport is the responsibility of another employer. For the most part the private stevedores undertake the shipwork and the PLA restricts itself to quay work (although there are variations from this pattern —see page 6).

The men also specialize. Those who work on board ship are called shipworkers, but they are also called stevedores. There are two unions in the enclosed docks, the Transport and General Workers' Union (T&G) whose members in the docks are known as dockers, and the National Amalgamated Stevedores and Dockworkers Union (NASDU), most of whose members work for the private stevedoring companies, and are therefore called stevedores.

Appendix II

Managerial Organization

The PLA has a docks office and a docks manager in each dock with general responsibility, not only for the dock work undertaken by the PLA, but also for the maintenance and servicing of the enclosed docks, of which the PLA is the landlord. In each sector cargo handling is allocated to departments, each of them with a senior traffic officer responsible to the docks manager. Traffic officers are in charge of the areas within the department, and the supervisors report to them.

Until 1970, in the South West India Department, foremen shipworkers, foremen quay gangers and shed foremen supervised the separate stages of the work with a labour foreman in each PLA department to allocate men to the traffic officers. In a reorganization in September of that year, following on the introduction of shiftwork, the PLA gave the new title of labour co-ordinators to the foremen quay gangers and some of the foremen shipworkers. Traffic officers and operational foremen now meet during each shift to work out each area's labour requirements for the following shift, and give them to the labour co-ordinators. These report shortages and surpluses to the departmental labour foreman, who tries to balance them between areas.

In the Millwall department the management organization has not changed. The PLA is responsible only for quay work there, and most of this is mechanized. There are no labour allocation meetings between the traffic officers and their shed foremen. Shed foremen notify the labour foreman directly of any requirements or surpluses they might have.

At the other two firms included in this study the senior managers were called superintendents and the supervisors were foremen or foremen shipworkers.

Under the casual system of employment, employers hired gangs organized by a member of the gang called the ganger. As leader of the gang he negotiated bonus payments with managers and in many instances played a part in the organizing of work. In a ship's gang, for example, the ganger might co-ordinate the work of the crane driver with the operations of the men in the hold and the gang on the quay. This responsibility was recognized by the employers who made a small additional payment to gangers. After September 1970 the PLA, along with some other employers, tried to include some gangers in the management team by distinguishing them unequivocally from other dockers.

Organizational charts illustrate the PLA's managerial structure before 1970 and afterwards.

P.L.A. Organization

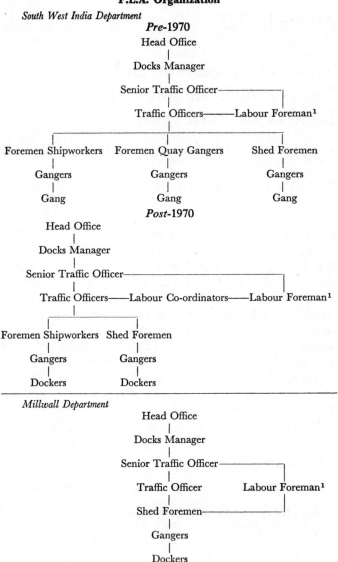

South West India Department

Pre-1970

Head Office
|
Docks Manager
|
Senior Traffic Officer————————————
| |
Traffic Officers————Labour Foreman[1]

┌──────────────────┼──────────────────┐
Foremen Shipworkers   Foremen Quay Gangers   Shed Foremen
| | |
Gangers   Gangers   Gangers
| | |
Gang   Gang   Gang

Post-1970

Head Office
|
Docks Manager
|
Senior Traffic Officer————————————————————
| |
Traffic Officers————Labour Co-ordinators————Labour Foreman[1]
|
┌──────────────────┐
Foremen Shipworkers   Shed Foremen
| |
Gangers   Gangers
| |
Dockers   Dockers

Millwall Department

Head Office
|
Docks Manager
|
Senior Traffic Officer——————————
| |
Traffic Officer   Labour Foreman[1]
| |
Shed Foremen———————————————————
|
Gangers
|
Dockers

[1] Labour foremen are not a superior grade of foreman. They are placed here in the organization chart only to indicate their role in labour allocation.

Appendix III

TGWU Organization and the Negotiating Committees in the London Enclosed Docks

The main negotiating body is the Enclosed Docks Joint Industrial Committee (EDJIC). Subordinates to it there are the Ocean Trades Group Joint Committee (OTGJC) and the PLA Group Joint Committee (PLAGJC). The T&G membership of the workers' side of the EDJIC consists of five full-time officers and two lay representatives, one of them elected by the Ocean Trades Lay Committee (OTLC) and the other by the PLA Lay Committee (PLALC). The TGWU membership of the workers' side of the OTGJC consists of up to three full-time officers and one lay representative, elected by the OTLC, and their PLAGJC workers' side membership is similar except that the lay representative is selected by the PLALC. The OTLC is elected by the relevant divisional committees, and the PLALC by the PLA stewards.

The TGWU organization in the docks is as follows :

Lay Committees	*Corresponding Full-Time Officers*
General Executive Council	General Secretary
National Docks Group Committee	National Docks Trade Group Secretary
No. 1 (London Region) Docks Committee	Regional Docks Trade Group Secretary
Divisional Committees	District Officers
Branches	

La Bibliothèque
Université d'Ottawa
Echéance

The Library
University of Ottawa
Date Due